LIVING THE LIFE

Memoirs of a Pimp's Life

BIG DAWG

iUniverse books may be ordered through booksellers or by contacting:

iUniverse
1663 Liberty Drive
Bloomington, IN 47403
www.iuniverse.com
844-349-9409

ISBN: 978-1-6632-4322-5 (sc)
ISBN: 978-1-6632-4323-2 (e)

Library of Congress Control Number: 2022914565

Print information available on the last page.

iUniverse rev. date: 08/05/2022

PREFACE

❖

In life your either going to be a hoe or a pimp one of the two. The essence of life is to be able to pimp yourself, being able to motivate yourself. When you don't have a lot of opportunities, then you gotta take chances.

A hoe has three feet, two on the ground and one in her ass. The third foot is motivation and that's what a pimp's job is. To motivate that person physically, mentally, spiritually, and culturally under the banner of the real and true pimp game.

People need to learn how to put that third foot in their own ass, so them themselves don't have to be pimped. I think all of us are prostitutes in some way or fashion because think about it, how many of us do absolutely what we want to do? When you give up a little bit of your integrity for whatever amount of money, you're a prostitute. If you work less and get paid more money than your employer, chances are, you too can pimp.

1

CHAPTER

❖

STARTING MY DAY BABY

I heard the beginning of a phone ring coming as clear as day from underneath a pile of clothes on the floor. I grabbed it before it could ring again "Hello," suspecting it to be one of my lady friends to see if I would be at home. "What's up nigga?" my patna Spark said in a harsh tone, sounding devious to the third power. "Blood its way too early to be calling me waking me up talking about what's up nigga like you insane." Now, Spark was a skinny dark skinned brutha with dreads in his hair with more bumps than a Seagram's gin bottle. He always wore the same clothes at least three times a week before changing into something different, despite not knowing how to talk to the ladies like I did. Spark was always known to get something cracking whether good or bad. "Awe man the early bird gets the worm nigga, you got to learn how to be the first muthafucka on the block for the cheese, and the last muthafucka to leave if you want to get money like me," answered Spark. I was just thinking to myself, this nigga always trying to throw how much money he got in my face, but it's cool, I ain't never been a playa hater I'm a "con-grad-u-later." I'm just glad his dirty ass is on my side to motivate me to get some of that good money. I said to him, "Check this out man, a playa needs his beauty sleep, vitamins, and protein, so that he can stay witty, and cunning with his game; he will know what to do and say with the ladies and have them bitches eating out the palm of my hand, ya dig Jack?" I could tell Spark thought to himself, this nigga thinks he Casanova or some dam body, always talking about what he needs to do to make his self-look good for these bitch's. Like I don't know how to talk to bitch's, man fuck this nigga I can't stand his bitch ass. Then Spark said to me, "You know I got love for you dawg, I love when you be talking that pimp shit but talking that pimp shit ain't gone put no money in your pocket or food in your stomach, so get your pimpin wannabe ass up

1

and let's get some money." Alright I said, but man I'm telling you this pimpin is gone pay me big one day Jack, and I ain't gone have to look or touch no dope ever again. All I'm gone have to do is talk shit, and swallow spit, to be the next Ghetto Donald Trump, too bad you ain't got a pimp bone nowhere in your body to get on the pimp space coaster to riches like I do". I laughed as he hung up the phone before Spark could respond. So, I got out of bed with my head in a fix and wondered dam, *"What am I going to wear today?"* I looked outside my window and saw the sun was out shinning nice and bright. I opened my closet and caught a whiff of one of my favorite colognes on the shelf in my closet. I contemplated on whether, I should wear a white T shirt, rockaware jeans, and my Nikes, or that brand new sky blue with the royal blue trim phat pharm sweat suit, that my lady friend "Kay-Kay" had bought for me last week for dicking her down. Kay-Kay is five two and her sexy thick self, is built like a gymnast. She has a caramel complexion, with brown eyes, and her hair was always in a small ponytail like she was going to do a somersault at a competition. Anyway, after a minute I decided to go with the phat pharm sweat suit, with the coke white Reebok shoes. I laid my clothes out on the bed, grabbed my boxer underwear, wife beater T-shirt and, left out through the bedroom door to go on my mission to procure some more money. When I stepped in the hall and headed toward the bathroom to take a shower, I heard, "Bitch! you are gonna have to stop fighting these other hoes on the track and start conducting yourself with some class and get a pimp his ration." My oldest brother said to his bottom bitch "T.T." My oldest brother is big, brown, six one, and two fifty, all mass and cut up. He wore a short haircut and a forever grin on his face. His girth is like the kingpin in Spiderman comics, and he had a slight bit of country ness to him when he talked. Anyway, T.T. had been his bottom bitch for years, she was a beautiful lady. She was light skinned, five foot four, with long sultry hair. Her body was scrumptious, with cantaloupe sized titties, a plump booty, and the prettiest light brown eyes in all of Oakland. I was reminiscing when she used to come in my room and rape me when my brother first knocked her nine years ago. I'm nineteen now, and that was a long time ago. It is what it is, but I wish she would try some shit like that now. I would show her ass that I wasn't scared of the pussy and let her feel how I'm a grown man now got dam it. "Daddy, I can't just let these other hoes push on me and get all the money, these bitches think I'm a punk on the track just because I'm prettier than their no dressing, insecure, jealous, wannabe me ugly asses. If I let them bitch's punk me daddy, we wouldn't be making no money at all." said T.T. "I know baby, but we can't afford to keep getting your hair fixed, nails done, and new clothes every time you get into a fight with these nothing ass bitch's out here. We have to save that money and recycle back into the game to step our game up, so you don't have to be out on that track taking penitentiary chances for us to get to the top," said my oldest brother. "Well daddy, what do you want me to do?" She responded in a sweet submissive voice with her eyes passionately looking at him. "Fuck it" he said, "From now on bitch, we gone fuck with the escort services and internets." As he got up and opened the door to his bedroom, he literally knocked me to the ground as he bumped into me accidently in the hallway because he was deeply in thought. He grabbed me before I could fall, being swift on his feet saying, "Sorry about that lil bro I didn't see you coming down the hall, what you about to do, jump in the shower?" Yeah! I said, "I gots to get dressed and go get this money on the block big brah so I can shine like you." My oldest brother looked at me with pride, and spoke on longevity and said, "lil brah, longevity is the only way you gone shine like me, I keep telling you the name of the game is to see who lasts the longest not who can make the quickest dolla. Ain't no longevity in that dope you selling out there in them streets, I told you, you need to jump in this pimp game, and do the things I been schoolin yo ass about." Who you doing your dope dealing thang wit? "Uh Spark" I said. "Spark! That ole ugly ass insufferable jealous ass nigga? Lil bro that dude ain't cool he gone fuck around and be the death of you. I know that's your homie and everything but, mark my words he is one of those undermining ass niggas that will get you caught up. It's just something about him that doesn't sit comfortable with me lil bro, watch yourself dealing with that low life snake ass nigga, be sure to dot your i's and cross your t's like I taught you… alright?" "Alright Big Bruh" I said as I continued my stroll to the bathroom. Big Bruh was on his way to the kitchen but just stared at me, with his penitentiary stares all the way till I closed the bathroom door. I looked at myself with the full-length mirror on the back of the bathroom door. I was admiring my amiable brown skin, coco complexion, one hundred- and eighty-five-pound sculptured body while brushing my low tapered haircut, with the waves all around my head. I was thinking to myself, *man, I gotta make sure I hit the nail shop to get a pedicure & manicure before I hit the block*. You never know what type of bitch you might meet coming through the neighborhood visiting family or, if you'll end up at the Hotel Suites for some sweet vicious penetrating sex. One of the things my big brother taught me was, "If you stay ready you ain't got to get ready" so stay getting ready so you will be already ready, and he would say after every smooth artistic slogan, church! The word church, in a pimp's terminology is, whatever speech you just said is not a lie and is ooh so real." When I opened the door to the bathroom and stepped back into the corridor, I ran into my second oldest brother. He stopped me in my tracks looking disgusting like he ain't took a bath in a week saying, "Big Dawg let me get a fifty rock on credit until I hit this lick later on tonight." My second oldest brother is five ten, milk chocolate, stocky build about two thirty, braided hair going backwards, and a look on his face that says I'm pissed. He affectionately called me Big Dawg because when I was in Junior High. I weighed two hundred and fifteen pounds and I was big, and chubby. Since I slimmed down to a cool one hundred and eighty-five, I've been on some high-power pimp shit. Everybody started calling me Big Dawg. "Dam bruh, you have the nerve while I'm walking through the hallway asshole naked to ask me for some dam credit. You couldn't have at least waited until I was finished washing my ass and dressed to hit me up?" While I stood face to face with my second oldest brother, looking into his eyes like we were getting the last instructions to commence a boxing match. I noticed they were big as golf balls. "Alright man its cool let me go hook it up for you" I slid past him to go hook up the fifty rocks for him and came back with a towel wrapped around my muscular body and handed him the dope. He did not say thank you, right on, or nothing as he sped off down the hall to the basement to free base his crack cocaine. I figured I may as well give it to him before he goes in my room and steal it himself and take way more than a fifty rock. My second oldest brother knew he could get away with it because, as soon as I would cause a commotion about my dope missing, he would run to mom's and put her in the middle of our drug pow wow. As usual, she would get upset and kick ME out of the house without a pot to piss in or a window to throw it out of. I thought to myself, *I gots to get my own apartment quick, so that I can have some peace of mind and tranquility, before I stress myself to death around here.* As I jumped in the shower and let the hot water run all over my body, I was nostalgic. I was thinking back when my second oldest brother wasn't a crack smoker, and he was a big-time drug lord distributing crack-cocaine all throughout the Oakland streets for about 10 years. He taught me how to cook up coke and turn it into crack. He taught me how to weigh up quarter ounces, half ounces, whole ounces, all the way up to a kilo of cocaine, on a triple beam scale. He even hooked me up with some of his previous connections before he started smoking. But now, I didn't need a triple beam scale to weigh my dope. Society has what you call a digital scale, something that is more modern with high technology to assist the latest dope dealer. All I had to do was count my figures and add up the profits. As my phone begin to ring in my room, I was coming back to reality. I already figured it was my boy Spark calling to complain on how long I was taking. So, I rushed lathering myself up with dial soap and jumped out of the shower. Dried off and looked out the bathroom door before fleeing to the bedroom, thinking to myself, *cool the cost is clear.* I trotted to the room and closed the door. I picked up the phone and looked at the caller ID to see who's call I had missed, and just like I thought, it was Spark calling. As I hurried up and put on deodorant, I put on my phat pharm sweat suit over the polo boxer briefs and the wife beater. I put on some white socks and coke white Reebok shoes, sprayed my cologne on, and headed toward the door. I was sharp as a tack! "Boy where you rushing off to in such a hurry?" Mom asked me as she stood here in the kitchen cooking breakfast. My mother is a short pretty brown put together woman, with Olympic pool shaped eyes. My mother knows how to get her point across by batting her eyes at you. If she were mad, happy, or sad you were going to know by the way she batted her eyes. "Don't you want some bacon, sausage eggs and home-made blueberry waffles?"

I contemplated it for a minute and responded, "Naw Ma, I have to hurry up and go pick Kay-Kay up and take her to this job interview in downtown Oakland. Can you save me a plate for when I get back a little later this afternoon?" My mother started batting her eyes like yeah whatever nigga tell me anything. She just smiled and said, "Sure, I can baby that's my son, always helping somebody when they need it." "Well come give momma a big hug and a kiss I barely get to see my boys anymore you guys are always so busy." I walked from the door over to mom and gave her a hug and a kiss putting five hundred on the countertop. "I love you mom; I love you too Baby" my mother said with a great big pretty white smile on her face! Just then I realized where I got my charm, cuteness, and wits from. "Alright moms I'm outta here" "Be careful she said, knowing I wasn't taking Kay-Kay to a job interview but wanting to believe it. I jumped into my candy green "whip" with the white stripes Chevy high performance Nova on rally rims and G.T. Qualifier tires. Proudly started up the engine and let the car idle for a while, then I put my platinum chain on with the diamond infested medallion and push the gas pedal to hear the cam and hooker headers breath through the flow master exhaust pipes. Feeling myself, I turned on the four twelve-inch woofers and amps to let the music spill out of the windows. A rap verse came through the Kenwood 6 Band Changer CD player saying, "Comin up we learn how to make these hoes and when you're through getting yours, then we shake these hoes." As I heard that verse, I got excited, shifted my Quick Silver stick shift in drive and burned rubber up the block on my way to pamper myself and possibly come up on a nice, sweet, petite, beneficial, pretty young thang, at the most popular nail shop in the town.

2
CHAPTER
❖
GOING FISHING

Pulling up to the nail saloon, I could see that I had an audience already of two pretty females looking out the window. Karen and her homegirl J.J. sat at the small cubicle by the window getting their hands and feet done talking girl talk. "Dam girl somebody is slamming hella heard!" J.J. said as she was looking out the window to see who was kicking the bass so hard it was raddling the windows. Karen said "That shit is to dam loud girl, I can't stand riding in a car with a nigga and his music is hella loud like that. A bitch could go deaf listening to that shit." J.J. didn't seem to be listening to her homegirl, because she was so curious and anxious to see who was slamming so hard. I pulled in front of the nail shop to get the attention of the ladies who were enjoying keeping their hygiene up and pampering themselves. When I looked to the right, I could see that I had an audience already of two pretty females looking out the window. This did nothing but challenge me to show off my charismatic aura. I shifted my candy apple green Nova into reverse, preparing to double park between two cars. While the Quick Silver shift stick was in reverse and the car rolling backwards, I hit the gas pedal slightly making my high profile G.T. Qualifiers screech the ground. I made them screech again, and again as I double parked between the cars in the first attempt perfectly. Knowing that all eyes were on me, I shifted the Quick Silver lever into park, turned up the music a few more notches. I let the car sit there and idle so that the women could hear my flow masters exhaust system mixed in with the music. I fired up a half of blunt that was in the ashtray and puffed on it. My music was still playing, and I was really feeling myself. "Dam Karen did you see how cute he was, he fuckin wit it ain't he?" Karen giving me the side eye said, "Yeah he was pretty cute, but he looks a little too young for me, but I would probably fuck wit him just to turn him out, and then leave his young ass white around the mouth." They both laughed. J.J. said, "Well which one is it big sis, is he too young to be on your level or do you want to turn him out?" "I don't know J.J. I been a hoe in the game for a long time! and you old enough to know not to judge a book by its cover." "For all we know, he may not be smart have any class, and be abusive." Karen said, "Well J.J. I'm going to give you a heads up if he is as cute as he was through the window in person, I'm going for what I know and may the best bitch win!" I was just finishing up half a blunt. I turned the music down and slightly hit the gas pedal a few times while the car was in park so the ladies could hear my dual flow master exhaust system before turning off the car. By this time Karen and J.J. were glued to the window while getting their hands and feet done. I stepped out the car making my chain swing so the sun could set the diamond off on my platinum medallion. I do that purposely so the diamond will glisten, while I make my grand entrance appear like I'm a star that I 'am. Walking towards the nail shop in a walk that showed complete confidence and assertiveness, then I glanced back at my car hitting the alarm button on the key ring. Slyly Giving warning that this car has state of the art security. "Look at him J.J., look at him" Karen said with a flabbergasted facial expression in awe. "Dam bitch I see him, you better get your composure together, the last thing you want him to notice is that you are infatuated by him". "Shh, shh, shh girl he is walking through the door." I walked through the door with this conceited attitude acting as if I didn't notice Karen and J.J. I knew they were watching me from the time I pulled up in front of the nail salon. The cologne mixed with the purple Cush I was smoking suddenly made the two beautiful women smile. As I noticed them smiling, I greeted them by saying a subtle, "How you ladies doing today?" Waiting for an answer, "Fine" they both said with their body language and behavior showing more than satisfaction. Karen was five seven, mocha colored, cute face, and had a body shaped like a bowling pen. You could tell she was a little bit older like late thirties or early forties because of the crow's feet next to her eyes. But she was still fine for an older woman. J.J. was like a mid-twenty-year-old, skin color like a caramel Frappuccino, shoulder length hair, curvy little brick house body, and a nice round face. J.J. had pretty brown innocent eyes and she was mixed with Hawaiian and Black. "How are you?" Karen emphasized in a seductive tone. "Worse than others better than most" me putting my Mack on her, making my voice sound deeper than usual. I asked were they sisters because they somewhat resembled each other. J.J. told me to guess which one was the oldest but I was like naw I'm cool I don't guess women ages. I was about to take a seat in the waiting area with the rest of the customers. Kimmie, the Asian owner, ran up to me grabbing my hand leading me in front of all of the other customers toward the largest seat and cubicle in the salon. It was like I was a rooster in a hen house! The customers looked at Kimmie and I with envy and admiration wondering why I got the royal treatment. Everybody was in shock because Kimmie never worked on anybody's manicure or pedicure. She would just assign one of her workers to do the job for her. Kimmie said, "Where have you been, me no see you long time how are you doing?" Then before I could answer she would say, "Good, yes? come I have seat for you already." Kimmie was in her forties with a nice body. She wore colorful outfits, but she was still hip. Her hair was bumped up real big kind of like a rock star from the eighties. Her face looked like a porcelain doll, but she wore thick eye shadow, and it was difficult to see her eyes. Her English was broken but still understandable. I stepped up to sit in the chair to get comfortable. When I took off my shoes and socks, Karen and J.J. stopped looking at me. They stared intentionally at my feet then looked at each other with the approval expression on their faces. J.J. turned to her older sister and said, "Girl I think I just found me a new pimp did you hear what he said, worse than others better than most? I love them slick talking, fast talking, players of the game." "J.J. calm yo ass down, dam girl! Said Karen "How do you know he is even a pimp; he might be just one of them dope dealing dudes that talk pimpin?" Well, if he ain't a pimp I'm gone make him a pimp" J.J. said. "Well go choose on his lil fine young ass then and stop playing before I beat you to the punch" Karen said. J.J. looking at her sister with gall says, "Not yet big sis you know it's all about timing when choosing a prospective pimp." "O.K. finish" one of the Asian employees told Karen and J.J. The two ladies dug in their purses and handed her a twenty-dollar bill each saying keep the change. The Asian lady frowned and said something in Chinese and rolled her eyes. Karen and J.J. didn't mind what she said they just said thank you and walked out the door. J.J. told her sister to wait in the car for a minute and she was going to holla at her soon to be daddy. When she walked back, she stood behind the wall peeping through the window. She saw me talking on my cellphone nonchalantly. "Spark man I said I'm on my way wardie, just chill out and hold it down till I finish getting my hand and feet buttered up." Spark said, "See that's the type of shit I'm talking about, you always putting that square shit in front of your riches. You could've been come through the block, dropped your worker of a couple of "G" bundles and got a few off yourself and been on your second round by now." So now I'm getting irritated, and I respond, "Well Spark let me tell you something, you listen, and you listen good. Understand me, first of all you have to treat yourself "not cheat" yourself. Second of all, it ain't about who can make the quickest dolla it's all about who can be around and last the longest to spend the dollars he made… church! I said that and hung the phone up in his face not giving him a chance to say anything as usual. "OK sir I finish, I do real good for you, O.K.?" Kimmie said. I pulled out a wad of money and gave her a twenty-dollar bill and tipped her a hundred dollars. "Thank you sir, you are so very nice, you good customer very long time, that why I rush to you and skip other customers." I told her that's what's up. "You hurry, I see girl keep looking in window for you to be her friend" said Kimmie. I peeped out the window and saw J.J. bringing her head back from the window trying not to be inconspicuous. "Kimmie, do you mind if I go out the back way to exit yo salon today?" Kimmie said, "No, you come you go I no care." "Thank you" I replied. So, I tip toed out the back door and came from around the build walking slowly and quietly to where J.J. was. When I passed by the car that Karen was sitting in, I winked my eye at her. She smiled with a look like dam dude is hella cute I should have hollered at him. I wonder if he has an older brother. Right when I got within arm reach of J.J, I said Boo! Not loud, not soft, but just enough to startle her. She jumped and gasped at the same time she turned around, "My God, you scared me." I said, "Ah baby I didn't mean to scare you I just wanted to surprise you" sticking my hand out at the same time she grabbed it. When she did, I introduced myself and kissed her hand and said, "My friends call me Big Dawg what yours?" My name is J.J., but my stage name is Sunshine." She answered trying to see if I understood the leisure underworld terminology and to let me know the kind of female she was. "Stage name? I said, Oh I see the game god has blessed me with honor of meeting a lady of leisure." Unphased, I said "Well then you should know what time it is when choosing a gentleman of leisure, its purse first and ass last" I said. Instantly, she started going in her purse and handed me a bunch of crumbled up twenty dollar and five-dollar bills. I didn't even count it as I put it in my pocket. I shook my head reluctantly and said, "Baby this is nowhere near enough." J.J. said, "I know daddy I have some more at home it's only about three thousand, I'll give it to you next time we see each other, OK?" I wanted to smile but I remembered one of the things my oldest brother taught me. I had to keep a cold stare, and never show emotions when it comes to getting your money from these bitches. Because if you smile, she will know that is the amount of money that will make **you** happy and **she won't** hustle harder to make more than what she just gave you. "OK baby that's cool that's cool, give me your phone number so I can hit you up later and see what it do." I said. She already had her number written down on a piece of paper and gave it to me. I looked at the number and put it in my pocket and started walking to the car pushing the alarm button on my key ring to turn the high-tech security alarm system off. It said alarm is disengaged please get in your car and drive safely. J.J. said, "Are you gonna give me your number baby?" I responded to her with a rhetorical smile and said, "Now pretty lady I'm not gonna give you my number just yet. In case you got some crazy ass jealous pimp who might sweat you when he sees you and find my number and try to start a pimp pow-wow before we even get off to a reputable jump start." I told her, "It's just precaution on my end baby, show me how sincere and loyal you are to me, and I'll give you the world "church!" as I jumped in the car and cranked the ignition vroom, vroom, vroom the car roared. As I rolled down the window I said, "Don't worry baby I'll call you later on this evening." "OK, I'll be waiting daddy" she said with a smile overwhelmed by the way I was handling her. With that said, I turned on my music, pumped the bass up a bit, shifted my Quick

Silver Shifter into drive, and drove off nice calm and cool. J.J. stood there and watched as I drove off, looking memorized and shit. She walked to the car where her sister Karen was waiting smiling at her little sister. Karen had witnessed the whole scene take place and J.J. sashayed her way to the car and they drove off.

3
CHAPTER
❖
HATING FROM AFAR

"**M**an, what the fuck is takin this nigga so long? I swear I can't stand his wannabe pimp ass he will never have money like me. When it comes to hustling, I runs circles around that fake ass nigga. If I wouldn't have grown up with this nigga, I would've been killed is punk ass." Said Spark. "Dam Spark" said one of the homies. I thought that was the patna, that's the way you feel about him? Spark answered irritated, "Hell yeah that's how I feel about him." Another one of the homies on the block said, "Man Spark, didn't he use to take up for you back in the day and made sure nobody fucked with you?" One of the homies on the block asked, "Don't he take life threatening and penitentiary chances to hold down the block? Don't he make sure none of these other tycoons take over our block, and have us buying dope from them?" His homie asked him, "And what about the time your pops had that stroke when you were out of town, didn't he stop what he was doing and rushed your pops to the hospital and stay by his side until you got back?" The little homies from the block told me all of the shit that Spark was saying when I wasn't around. Spark lashed out and said, "Man I don't give a fuck what dat nigga did for me, my family, or this block, that's what I do, I use niggas as pawns and deceive they asses in the end to the best of my interest I don't give a fuck about nobody but myself. You need to take notes from me little nigga and maybe you will learn something." He stated this in a disrespectful vicious tone with his fists clenched as if he was about to "open-up" a can of whoop ass on the little homies. Because the homies from the block was giving me my props and admiring my loyalty to the block. Spark would speak of me in an acrimony's way if anybody every brought me up to him. So, the little homies just left it alone and didn't say anything. I knew he needed me more than I needed him. One of the homies put his head down and jogged to the stash where his bundle of dope was. He put a few of the wrapped-up substances in his mouth and continued to "get his money on." "I am taken notes," one of the homies said under his breath, but I ain't takin none from you. Spark was a hater from afar, and I didn't want to believe it. I pulled up to the block and got out of my car. Spark was the first one to run up and give me a hug and a handshake saying, "Man you gone live a long time, I was just talking about you to Dee. Dee was five feet three inches tall and always wore a sports team hat to the back. He was a young black teenager that wore baggy jeans and sports hoodies. His face was always solemn, and he listened hella good to the OG's. Spark nervously urged Dee to tell me how you are my hommie and how much love I got for you." "Thanks Spark, you already know you my nigga as much as I been there for you and your family. I know you feel the same about me. I walked past Spark and gave Dee some dap. Dee said, "What's up Big Dawg that phat pharm sweat suit you got on go, where you get that shit at?" I responded, it's all on a bitch my young nigga, it's all on a bitch." See that's what I'm saying man a nigga got to be able to get it at all four corners not just selling dope," said Dee. "When you get older Dee, if you want, I will school you on the characteristics of how to be a full-blown player. You definitely have a pimp bone in you, you just need somebody to give you a push." Gushing with pride he said, "I would be honored to be following in your footsteps big brah," Spark rolling his eyes interrupts and says, "Enough with the sentimental ass kissing, Dee get yo ass across the street and serve some of them knocks before I raise your bitch ass up off the block!" Turning his agitation to me and says, "And as for you Big Dawg, that's my worker not yours. You need to go see what's up with one of your workers because I think he's out of work" I rubbed my lower lip and chin at the same time and looked at Spark contemplating if I should say something about how he just embarrassed the home boy Dee. I decided against it and walked to the front porch where "Dave baby" was sitting. Dave baby is six foot tall, dark, always wearing his beanies pulled down past his eyebrows. He wore dark clothes that looked worn. Dave-baby was my worker, but I didn't refer to him as a worker. I referred to him as my partner. I knew how to treat my workers and cared about what they were trying to be later on in life. Spark, on the other hand didn't give a shit about his worker's or what they were going through. One time Dee came up fifty dollars short on one of his G bundles and Spark got his forty-four Chrome Desert Eagle. He pointed it at Dee and put him in the trunk of his beat-up ass Monte Carlo. On purpose, He drove up to the skyline hills and told one of the homies to get out with him and they pistol whipped Dee until he was half conscious. Then they made him strip bucked naked and left him there in the middle of the street in the cold. He had to walk back three miles to get home.

4
CHAPTER
❖
SCRATCH MY BACK

"What's up Dave-baby?" I said while extending my hand to give him some dap. "How are your moms and Grandma doing?" I said. "They are doing cool my mom's just came back from the hospital from having a seizure and my grandma is in the kitchen making her famous Cajun fried catfish for us to eat on." I would always ask Dave-baby about his moms and grandmother first. I knew not worry about Dee's little sister and his grandfather. I knew how sensitive he was about his mother and grandmother being crack smokers, so I don't bring it up. Plus, I liked to talk to him about his family off top, before conducting business with him. "Well, I'm going to go inside your crib and say hi to your moms and grandma before I give you another G bundle alright?" He gave me a head nod and we walked to the house. As I walked up the porch and opened the door the whiff of the good home cooked Cajun fish hit me in my nostrils. "Dam D. that fish is smelling hella good" I said while sliding Dave-baby grandmother two twenty-dollar bills and a fifty-piece rock. She took the money and the fifty-piece rock, and put it in her bra and said, "Thank you, I will smoke this crack later on tonight but right now I'm drinkin this Tonk Gin straight so I can get fuuuucked UP!" I affectionately called her momma joe. Her skin was like dark chocolate, four foot four, always rocking an apron and had a Mississippi twang from the south. "Ah shit" I said, "I know what that means, somebody is going to get cussed the fuck out tonight." Momma joe just started laughing while I went upstairs. I went upstairs to see how Dave-baby's mom El-boogey, was feeling after coming back from the hospital. Before I could get all the way to the top of the stairs El-boogey opened the door. El-boogey is five three with a slim build like Jay Jay from Good times. She looks like she was rescued from being shipwrecked while wearing a head rag. "Can I get a hit Big Dawg?" She said looking literally half dead. "I answered, didn't you just come from the hospital from having a seizure? I told you, you need to chill out on that crack for a few months and get to one of those sober living environments to get your shit back together." "I know" she said, "but its hard Big Dawg, this crack is the devil himself. "I want to quit, but I just can't stop smoking it, I think I would rather die before I stopped smoking crack." I felt a chill run through my spine, after I heard that I knew El-boogey was never going to a sober living environment and that she would die being a dope fiend. I saw how desperate she looked and sympathetically passed her her daily medicine which was two twenty-dollar bills and a fifty rock. she said, "Thank you" unlike my second oldest big brother. She excepted her daily allowance and walked back in her room and nestled herself on the floor to smoke her crack pipe. I took a deep breath and prayed to God silently, *please God show me another way to make a dollar.* As I was reminiscing about not knowing anything about drugs when I was a little boy while washing my hands, I think I heard a knock on the bathroom door "Who is it?" I said, "Its Ivory she snapped." Dave-baby little sister yelled through the door "I have to change my maxi pads can you hurry up and finish so I can use the bathroom?" Ivory was brown skinned late teens, skinny like string beans and always wearing a head rag and pajamas in public. No fucks giving with her house shoes on like nigga what?! "Ivory, now you know that was too much information to be telling me. I'm coming out right now." So, I finished washing my hands but couldn't find a towel nowhere in sight. I dried my hands with toilet paper then opened the door. She was standing there looking like she needed to shower up, and in some raggedy ass pajamas with a scarf on her head and some house slippers exposing her dirty ass toes with chipped paint on her toenails. I dropped her a twenty and told her to get her feet and hands done. I passed by her headed back down the stairs.

I came down to the bottom of the stairs and the man of the house greeted me. Mr. Lock was a shiny black man, about five foot nine, WWII vet, bow legged, still in nice shape for an old man that rocked his suspenders always with polished shoes. Mr. Lock had a stack of envelopes in his hand and handed them to of all people, me. While rubbing the top of his already thin salt and pepper hair he says, "These bills are due by the 5th of this month" with a sinister grin on his face. I told him "No problem" feeling that was the least I could do for this family while me and the crew sold drugs on their property. They scratch my back and I scratch theirs. Spark didn't do shit for his family while we made money on their premises. As I was about to break Mr. Lock off some money, I realized he gets money from his Social Security check and a disability voucher. I also remembered Mr. Lock has more money than everybody put together. After I looked the bills over and went out the door, I yelled back at Mr. Lock. I told him I would get his lawn done for him and have somebody clean up the front and back patio. "You ready for another G bundle?" I asked Dave-baby. "I stay ready big brah, shoot me as many G bundles as you can, I need to try and get the hell up out of this shit hole! I need to get my own place to live before this muthafucka burns to the ground." I would pay Dave-baby one hundred out of every G bundle he ran through, unlike Spark who would only give Dee two hundred a day. On the block you could run through a G bundle in an hour, that's why Dave-baby loved the way, I paid him because he would stay out making money for at least 8 to 10 hours a day. A hundred dollars an hour added up to eight hundred or one thousand a day for Dave-baby. While Dee stayed outside for 12 hours a day and only get two hundred from Spark. Who wouldn't want to work for me and make a hundred dollars an hour? I said, "OK Dave-baby, let me call this bitch house and have her bring me some more dope out of my stash."

5
CHAPTER
❖
MY FAITHFUL RIDE OR DIE CHICK

I stood on the corner and sold dope, only when I was doing bad. Other than that, I would have my clientele call my cellphone only at night. "Hello," a seductive excited voice sounded over the phone. "Kay-Kay what's up baby how's the beautiful love of my life doing?" I said. Kay-Kay is light skinned, five foot ten, with an asymmetric hairstyle with blonde highlights. She has a petite build with apple sized titties, nice perfectly shaped bumble bee ass, and a big naughty smile that's hella sexy and attractive to a nigga. She answered, "I'm doing fine baby, when am going to see you?" I said, "That's what I was calling you about, come to the block so we can smoke a few blunts and do a little bumping and grinding?" She said, "O.K. baby let me put my shoes on and I'll be on my way." I said, "O yeah baby, bring me ten G bundles so I can distribute a few out and take back to da house." It sounded like she felt a little uneasy because she knew the only reason why I'd called her was about bringing me my dope. Plus, I didn't want to drive halfway across town I would make her ass do it for me, she ain't tripping. She didn't mind at all because she knew she would be able to see me, and that was one of the main reasons she let me keep my work at her house. "OK baby" Kay-Kay said while she got her shoes and, the ten G bundles for her favorite man. Right when she was backing out of the driveway, her boyfriend Boo popped up unannounced, "Bitch where you think you going?" Boo hating ass jumping out of his car and blocking her driveway so she couldn't move. Boo is a six one, black ass pudgy ass nigga, that gives of Sonny Liston vibes. He is hella jealous and protective and his clothes looks like he's been under cars doing oil changes for decades. But homeboy got money so that's why she fucks with him. She gathered her nerves and answered, "Hi Boo I was just on my way to the grocery store to buy a few things for the house." His skeptical ass responds, "Are you always this happy when you're on your way to the dam grocery store?" Trying to brush off his verbal assaults she says, "Come on baby is that anyway to talk to your future wife?" I was thinking about you that's why I was so happy that you surprised me." Boo just smiled and attempted to open her car door, "Can I have a little affection before you leave baby, I'm feeling a little emotional?" Unwillingly she got out the car, pumped herself up, and gave Boo a hug and a kiss. She said to herself, *"Dam, I hate letting this ugly fat muthafucka hug and kiss on me. I can't wait until Big Dawg really decides to give me his one hundred percent so I can leave Boo insecure ass. But that's the price I got to pay for him paying my rent, car-note and all my bills because Big Dawg ain't gone pay shit for a bitch."* When Kay-Kay finished giving Boo some love and affection she said, "O.K. baby let me get to the grocery store before it gets to crowded and I be stuck in there all day." Boo said, "Alright baby be careful," then said in a forceful angry voice, "And you bet not be fuckin around with that punk ass nigga Big Dawg!" Smiling nervously, she wondered in her mind, *"Dam where in the hell did, he get that from?"* She regrated telling Boo about me. She only did it to make him stay on top of his game. Trying to do her best Oscar nominee performance she yells, "Fuck dat nigga I told you I don't mess with that fake ass nigga. I love you Boo, and nobody else. He is the last nigga you got to worry about!" She backed her car out of the driveway and sped off. She phoned me to tell me about her little dust up with Boo and how everything went down after she safely drove off from the house. Kay-Kay pulled up to my block in East Oakland smiling at me while she parked her car. Out the corner of my eye, I spied Spark standing in the cut looking at Kay-Kay with a pleasing to the mind facial expression that read if only he could have her. She got out the car to meet me, her favorite man, with a touch of lips pressing against my lips before I could say anything to her. I said, "Whoa I see somebody's happy to see me. How's my pretty lady doing today?" She clutched me holding on for dear life. She answered, "I was feeling kind of neglected, but I'm fine now that I get to spend a little quality time with my favorite man." *I would always wonder what the hell did she mean by saying her favorite man* like she got a roster of niggas to choose from. I didn't sweat it too much. I was taught to not sweat these hoes, and let these hoes, because you don't own them, and they are going to do what they want to do with or without you. I beckon for Kay-Kay to get in the car so that I could receive the ten-thousand-dollar bundle. I needed to get it into the hands of Dave-baby as quickly as possible before five O, hit the corner and Jack the shit out of them. We sat in the car, and she handed me the plastic bags with the dope inside. "Dave-baby check it out!" I spoke. He ran over to where I was and stood by the car and stuck his head inside the window. "What's up big brah?" Then I said, "How many bundles you think you can handle today?" Dave-baby said, "You can shoot me... All of that shit big brah! You already know I'm on a mission to get my own place and a new car!" I smiled at him and admired his optimistic attitude about "hustling" for a cause to reach his goals. "Alright lil brah then peep game, and check play. I'm gone split the bundles up with you ya dig? Now take five and I take five, because I'm gone need some to take to the house and serve some of my personal clientele on the late night is that cool?" "Ay man its however you want to do it big brah, you're the boss just hurry up and give it to me so I can put it in my stash before the police hit the corner and catch us being dirty" said Dave-baby. I counted out five G bundles and handed it to Dave-baby and he took off in a flash and was running like he was getting chased by dogs to stash his half of the dope. I turned to Kay-Kay and said, "You ready to smoke a few blunts with your favorite man with a sarcastic voice?" She turned to me in a coaxes gesture knowing I was on to her favorite man slogan, but she didn't trip. "Yes baby, do you have some weed already or do we have to go to the weed spot and get some?" she said. "I just smoked my last half of blunt before I went inside the nail shop to get buttered up, we got to go to the weed spot." Then she started her new 2007 Altima and drove off.

6
CHAPTER
❖
THE TROJAN HORSE

When we pulled up to the weed spot I told her, "Baby you know these niggas ain't gone give me a good deal for this hundred I'm about to spend, won't you get out and do your hips lips and fingertips vanity routine on these trick ass niggas?" "O.K anything for you baby" Kay-Kay responded in a submissive tone. It was time for me to deploy my "trojan horse trick" to get what I wanted. The "trojan horse" trick is I send her in first. The Greeks pretended to sail away, and the Trojans pulled the horse into their city as a victory trophy. That night, the Greek force crept out of the horse and opened the gates for the rest of the Greek army, which had sailed back under cover of night. The Greeks entered and destroyed the city of Troy, ending the war. So, I use Kay-Kay to get me in and then I clean them niggas out for little or nothing. Say playa, don't hate me, hate the game. Anyway, she stepped out of the car walking to where the weed boys were standing and blurred out, "Who can give me the best deal for my hundred dollars" showing an intrepid attitude. One youngsta ran up and said, "I can give you five fat twenty sacks for your hundred dollars!" Kay-Kay looked at him and said, "That ain't no deal little boy what you tryna do, make your daily quota off me?" She turned around with an attitude and said, "Where the niggas at who run this block?" Finally speaking up like roll call in school dude raised his hand and said, "That would be me." He is an obese charcoal colored O.G. dude eating a twenty-piece bucket of chicken from Popeyes. Time for Oscar nomination time, Kay-Kay whined sounding like a sweet innocent little child. "Can I get ten twenty sacks for my last one hundred dollars big daddy?" She was pumping his ego and self-esteem up. Grumpily he replied, "Can I have your phone number?" Startled at first but she kept up the act and said, "Of course, you can big daddy, if you give me ten twenty sacks for these hundred dollars you can have more than that!" That really put some spunk in the charcoal colored O.G. vibe. He got up and went to his stash spot while she wrote a fake number down. He came back and gave her fifteen twenty sacks. She grinned while she excepted the fifteen bags of weed and handed him the fake phone number she wrote on a napkin and kissed it before giving it back to him. He started blushing and feeling fluttery while he looked at her with familiarity in his face. She said "You better call me too big daddy" then she started walking away quickly before he recognizes her from giving him the wrong number from her last visit to his weed spot. Kay-Kay got into the car and gave me all fifteen bags of the weed showing her loyalty and honesty like she always did. I looked at the bags of weed in amazement and said, "Dam I knew I could trust in you to come thru Kay-Kay, see what a little charm and manipulation will do for you?" She answered, "Yes baby I will do anything for **you,** all you got to do is tell me what to do and I'll do it with no questions asked." I said, "Do you really expect me to believe that?" Then she said, "I can show you better than I can tell you." Shaking my head in agreement I said, "Well let's get the hell out of here for starters and drive extra careful, cause I'm dirty as fuck." I told her to take me back to the block so that I can jump in the Nova and follow her back to her spot. She started the car and drove away from the weed spot to the block so that I could get into my car and follow her home.

7
CHAPTER

❖

COOKING LIKE A CHEF

We arrived at my drug infested neighborhood and Spark was casually standing on Dave-baby's porch. With a resentful expression he was watching me as I got out of Kay-Kay's car and into my candy green Nova. He caught her attention and blew her a kiss. She turned her nose, frowned at Spark, and started driving off with me following her to her house. When I got to her house, the first thing I did was check my stash. I counted twenty thousand dollars cash, a kilo, and a half of cocaine, and fourteen one-thousand-dollar G bundles. Not to mention what I had in my car that I would sell later on that night. I wasn't thinking about nothing else but my money. I was on hella focused and on top of my game. When I finished, I gave Kay-Kay a pack of philly blunts and five twenty sacks and told her to roll up the weed. I figured I might as well cook up the other half of that kilo while I was still here. I put on a pot of boiling hot water grabbed a fresh bowl some arm and hammer baking soda, and my Pyrex bowl. I crushed up the half kilo with the bottom of the Pyrex bowl until the dope turned into a powdery form. I retrieved my digital scale and started weighing the arm & hammer baking soda and mixed the dope and baking soda together in a big brown paper bag and started shaking it together like I was shaking flour to fry some chicken. By this time the water was boiling hot. I put the mixed substance into the Pyrex bowl and put the bowl into the pot simmering the fire on the stove till the fire was slow bringing the pot of water to a slow boil. I was cooking my shit up like a bonafide chef! While I was handling my business in the kitchen, Kay-Kay saw this as an opportunity to call Boo from a restricted phone number to see where he was so she wouldn't get caught up. Not that I would mind, it was Boo she had to worry about. She went in the room while she still rolled the weed to get her phone and dialed Boo's cell number. "Hello" a raspy harsh out of breath voice answered, "Hey baby I was calling to tell you I was going to stop by mother's house before I came home, okay?" said Kay-Kay. "Alright baby you better have your ass home in the next couple of hours because I want some of that red bone pussy." "*Fuck!*" She whispered to herself not wanting to have sex with him. "Sure thing baby, I'll be waiting and ready when you get here. She finished rolling up the weed and went into the living room and fired up a blunt then passed it to her favorite man. I was admiring my dope closely cook, and I took a few puffs of the blunt and started choking. "Shit," I said as my eyes started to water. "That's that good purple "Cush" then passed it back to her. "How long do you think you gone be daddy before you are finished cooking up your dope?" asked Kay-Kay. "Well baby when I finish cooking this shit up, I'm going to have to cut it into G bundles so I can flood Dave-baby with it" I said. I looked at her and said, "Why what's up?" She stated that she needed to go to the grocery store and pick up a few things for the house before they closed, plus she wanted some of that fire dick that I be holding between my legs." Looking at her with a smirk I said, "Now Kay-Kay, you know you ain't getting none of this fire dick from me until you show me how much I mean to you." Dam she said, "fuck it, it was still worth a try" and she said, "I just gave you that new phat pharm suit you are wearing." But I told her, "Baby this was two weeks ago I need something else that's up to date you know what I'm saying?" She started getting aroused by the way her favorite man was conducting himself. "No problem daddy, no problem I will have some money for you the next time I see you." She told me that she was thinking how much money to ask from Boo to give her, after he finished fucking her with his deformed thumb size dick. I looked at my dope cooking again and could see it was cooked to the oil and was ready for some cold water to shock it, so it could turn hard as nails. After I finished running cold water over the Pyrex bowl, I shook it out and it all came out in one fat cake looking cookie. My mouth watered to see how much extra dope I had made from the 18-ounce half of kilo. I dried the dope while puffing on another blunt Kay-Kay had sparked up. I put it on the scale, it read 22 ounces and fourteen grams I smiled and said, "I love it when a plan comes together." See I had learned how to stretch powder coke, by turning it into crack from my second oldest brother. I loved my second oldest big Bruh for teaching me that method. By learning that method, I earned an extra forty-nine coming out the pot. I sat down and cut the crack cocaine into twenty-two one thousand G bundles and put it with the other whole kilo and twenty thousand dollars cash. I would never worry about selling weight as long as I had a block that pushed crack. Kay-Kay and I finished smoking the blunts, and I started to leave. Right when I grabbed the door, she threw herself on me. She was desperately begging for me to give her some of that sweet meat that I had between my legs. I kept my composure by not giving into her spell. She said, "Well then can I just suck it for you daddy?" I thought for a minute and said, "Fuck it baby gone ahead and suck it." As she got on her knees and opened her mouth, I pulled down my sweatpants and pulled my already hard manhood out then sat back down. I started talking dirty to her the way she liked it saying, "Yeah bitch suck that dick for daddy, suck that dick for daddy, you like the way the dick taste in your mouth don't you, get it nice and went baby, nice and wet!" After fifteen minutes of her slurping stroking and sucking I busted my load in her mouth. She stroked harder and faster to make sure she got every bit of my love potion and swallowed all my babies not leaving a drip. She just let my manhood marinate in her mouth for an extra three minutes like she was savoring my shit. When I was finished, I pulled my sweatpants up and exhaled, just then she jumped up and thanked me for letting her suck my dick and she wiped it off for me. I told her to be good and to stay down with me as I walked out the door feeling like a king.

8
CHAPTER
❖
A CLOSE CALL

As I pulled up to the block, my boy Dave-baby walked up and said, "I'm almost finished big brah, I only have two G bundles left." I looked at him with bliss and admired him for his hustle. "Like that?" I said. "Well, I might as well give you the rest of the bundle that I have on me." Dave-baby had an optimistic and positive attitude, and I didn't mind giving him extra. The little homie was on a mission. He has his goals of getting his own apartment and a new car and I'm trying to help him do that. I handed Dave-baby the dope, and Spark came out the alley being boisterous for no apparent reason that I could see. "What's up mane?" you give that lil nigga a few more bundles?" said Spark. I responded, "Yeah why, and what you all in my business for, worry about what you and your worker not me and mines, ain't that what you told me earlier?" Spark responded "Dam, brah, I didn't mean to offend you why you being all sensitive on a nigga? "You coming out the ally like you trying to check a nigga being hella loud and shit like you wanna see me about something." I spoke sternly. Spark said, "Aah my bad, I just been drinking this pint of Remy while you were gone." I changed the subject because I saw that he toned his voice down and talked to me with some respect. I said, "Man its gone be popping at the club tonight we fuckin wit it?" I don't have nothing to wear" said Spark with a pathetic look on his face. "Nigga, you make all that money and pay your worker crumbs and don't buy shit, you need to start living a little bit when you die you can't take none of that Shit with you." I said. He said, "Don't worry about what I do with my money, I'm just not into 'flossing' and being flamboyant like you, that's why I stay having more paper than you." "It seems like you always try to belittle me every day telling me how much money you have." "I'm like this cause I like to have things to show for what I'm doing and to let muthafucka's know what the turf is worth if somebody was on the outside looking in". "It would look like I had way more money than you." I said. Spark said, "Blood, I'm not trying to knock how you carry yourself, but doing all that "stuntin" will attract the wrong kind of people. It could attract the police, some niggas trying to 'jack you' or worse. Somebody might want to kill you!" I told him, "A moving target is hard to hit plus if some niggas try to fuck with me all I have today is hit the gas and let the Nova leave they ass in the dust. The only way somebody could get at me is if it was someone that knew me." Completely acquiescing, "Alright Big Dawg I give up you win, can you take ya boy to get something to wear for the club tonight or what?" Spark said. Not tripping off of nothing I said, "Anything for my best patna, jump yo dusty ass in the car and let's hit Oxford Street at Bay Fair Mall." Maybe I can knock me a few bitches while we out splurging." I gave him a pack of philly blunts to roll up some more weed. That's the weed that I got from the weed spot that ole girl had manipulated. She had the big charcoal colored O.G. mesmerized. I turned on my sound system and blasted off to the 580 freeway to Bay Fair Mall. When we pulled into the parking lot, we sat in the car to finish smoking weed. We noticed some dude around the same age as us, and dude kept on staring. Dude was sitting in a beat-up ass Chevy Nova like mine except, mine was cleaner than his. Dude got out the car and looked at Spark and I with a look that would kill. He headed toward the entrance of the mall and kept staring at us. Spark said, "Ay brah why don't we go to another mall and go shopping for what we gonna wear to the club tonight?" I said, "Man fuck that its hella bitches in the mall shopping for shit to wear this weekend, you know how those hoes get when they get their welfare checks and spend it all on themselves and don't by their kids shit." Spark didn't want to tell me the reason why he wanted to go to another mall and not Bay Fair. He didn't want to make himself seem like a punk in my eyes. So, when we finished smoking blunts, we got out the car and headed toward the same entrance the dude in the raggedy Nova went into. Inside the mall, I turned the volume up on my star, charismatic, talking loud, bag carrying, popping tags self. Spark had a few bags and was quiet like a bookworm reading a dam book. He was leery of that dude that he saw go into the mall before us. I wasn't tripping, I was talking to every chick in the mall moving. I told Spark that I got my bullet proof vest on, in case some of these bitches want to shoot me down "church!" Spark was encouraging me to hurry up so that we could leave the mall, but I was having too much fun, getting numbers, and interacting with the ladies. Then he said, "I bet Dave-baby is almost finished with them G bundles" in a facetious way. I regained my composer thinking about my money. I said "O yeah, I almost forgot I gave Dave-baby those extra bundles. Let's hurry up and get back to the turf. Leaning into Spark I said, "Am I tripping or does that grimy looking nigga keeps following us?" Spark turned to see who I was talking about. You could tell that the butterflies hit his stomach as soon as he saw the dude that was in the beat-up ass Nova that looked at us with death in his eyes. Rubbing his stomach Spark said, "Naw Big Dawg you ain't tripping, that dude was looking at us like he knew us when we first walked in." Fed up I said, "Well I'm gonna see what's up with this nigga you coming?" I could see Spark wasn't showing any confidence. So, I said, "Fuck it just chill while I see what's up with this buster ass nigga." I walked toward the dude in the raggedy Nova with pure vengeance on his face and said, "What's up nigga you got a muthafuckin problem or something?" Dude in the raggedy Nova said with his hands up "Naw Big Dawg I ain't gotta problem I was just admiring you and ya boy popping at the bitches and buying up the mall. With a devilish devious grin, I said "Well punk ass nigga you need to fall back and let me and my homie breath in this muthafucka before I "Flame" yo ass like smokey." Then dude in the Nova said, "Alright Big Dawg it's your world I'm just walking through it" and walked ahead of us. We followed him all the way out the mall. When we got in the car I said, "Man you a straight coward I thought you would've stepped to dude with me!" I would've thought you was hard the way you be beating up on the little homies in the hood or are you just hard toward people you know?" Spark had nothing to say because he was really spooked of dude in the Nova for no reason whatsoever. While we were on E 14th driving toward the 580 Freeway to get back to the turf, dude in the raggedy ass Nova pulled up on the side of us and said, "What's up with that shit you was talking up in the mall Big Dawg, what up now huh?! What's up now huh?! Then I yelled to him, "Pull yo ass over nigga, pull yo ass over nigga!" Dude in the raggedy ass Nova motioned for me to go in front of him. Right when I pulled over and stepped out the car to fight dude, he pulled out a stainless steel nine-millimeter and shot six times. I fell to the ground not knowing whether I was hit or not, and dude sped off. Spark sat there looking shocked, but I was relieved when I saw that I didn't have any bullet holes in me and only a little grease and dirt on my sweat suit. Grateful that dude was a no aiming ass nigga I hurried up and jumped back into my car. That was a close call. I asked Spark if he was alright, and he shook his head up and down to let me know that he was okay. My nose turned up and I said, "What the fuck is that smell" and looked at him for an answer. That's when I noticed he had shitted his pants and I busted up laughing saying, "Dam nigga you done shit on yourself?" then he said, "I couldn't help myself, my stomach got queasy when we were in the mall, and we first seen dude." Trying to stop laughing I said, "Well blood try not to get that shit on the interior of my car" and Spark said, "I won't Big Dawg just don't tell anybody what I did alright?" I knew not to say anything to a soul because Spark had a reputation to uphold, then I responded, "It's all good, I won't tell nobody as long as you be cool with that bullshit, smashing on the youngsters' and being a bully." Spark agreed then we rode from E 14th to go to the 580 Freeway so we can go back to the hood in East Oakland. When we got back to the block, Spark sprung out of my candy green Nova and ran up the porch to Dave-baby's bathroom. With shopping bags in his hands from the mall full sprint. Dave-baby handed me five thousand dollars and said, "What's wrong with Spark he was running like he had ants in his pants?" I said, "He had something in his pants but it sure wasn't ants." Trying not to be obvious with the way I was laughing. As I began to count my money to make sure the money was straight. I handed Dave-baby five hundred dollars then he smiled at me and told me he would be finished with the other five G bundles later on tonight. I told him I was going to the club later and that I would be back to check on him later that night. We gave each other some dap, and I drove off. Spark came back out of the house in a new outfit and asked Dave-baby where his worker Dee was at. He ignored Spark as he walked to his stash to put some more rocks in his mouth. Spark watched Dave-baby attentively as he watched and saw where his stash was located. While Dave-baby was busy serving the dope fiends in the neighborhood, Spark went to Dave-baby's stash and stole my dam five G bundles. So, he thought that I would beat Dave-baby ass and all of the money could go to him. When he went back to his stash spot, he was devastated to find that the dope was missing. He asked Spark if he had seen anybody where his dope was hidden. Spark gave him the silent treatment like he received from him thirty minutes prior to him asking where Dee was at. Dave-baby had a feeling either Spark took it, or he knew who did. Frustrated he had no proof Spark took it, he wondered walking to the house thinking how he could explain what happened to me.

9
CHAPTER
❖
SHIT, DAM, MOTHERFUCKER

I decided to put my Nova in the garage because of the incident earlier with dude in the raggedy ass Nova. I knew my car was hot now and wanted to be more inconspicuous. I'd bring the Nova back out when we went to the club. My cellphone rung, "Hello?" "Baby I have some money for you" Kay-Kay told me." "Cool baby I will swing through there and pick it up before I go to the house and park the Nova," I spoke. She said, "I'll be waiting daddy and be ready to dick me down when you get here." I told her, "Make sure it's nice and fresh baby because I'm ready to be as nasty as I wanna be." Then hung up the phone. I pulled up to her house, a big dark-skinned brother with razor bumps on the back of his neck looking like pieces of old chewing gum was getting in his truck and drove away from in front of her house. I figured that must've been one of her lil trick friends she used to pay her bills. I got in the house and asked, "Who was that big fat baboon looking ass nigga coming outta the house?" She answered, "The nigga whose money I'm about to give you!" I cracked a smile like a Cheshire cat and told her to get in the shower because her favorite man was about to give her a marathon fucking. When she returned, I was chilling and waiting in my birthday suit. She dug into her purse and gave me one thousand five hundred dollars cash. It was the money she got from Boo thang for letting him hump on her with his thumb sized dick. She dropped to her knees soaking wet ready to indulge in her professional dick sucking tactics. But I said. "Baby this one is on me" then I picked her up, holding her by her ass and slide my manhood in her. As I pounded inside her walls, thrust after thrust, she started moaning and saying my name. "Big daddy, big daddy, oh shit, this is my favorite dick, this is my favorite dick!" Then I brought her to the kitchen table and eased my dick out of her throbbing wet pussy. As the sweat was dripping down my chest like the drops were racing.

I told her, "Lay back and put your legs up over my shoulders." I buried my head between her legs licking her clit and sucking on it like I was trying to suck out her soul. My tongue was moving rapidly on her clit that with every stroke it made her stomach jump. She rubbed the top of my head with her hands like an owner petting his dog. I was sucking and licking her clit slowly, I started easing my finger in her ass inch by inch taking it slow. She immediately started grinding her pussy on my face grabbing her breast at the same time. I was driving her mad and right when she screamed, she was coming, I put my mouth on the opening of her walls and sucked the cum out of her pussy. My fingers were still between her ass cheeks, and I swallowed all of her love potion. I removed my head from between her walls and motioned for her to get off the table and face the wall. She acquiesced fast and I slide my manhood in her from behind. At that moment, I started talking dirty to her saying, "Yeah baby big dick baby, big dick baby, you gone get me some more money baby, you gone get daddy some more money baby?" She answered with a hysterical nirvana speech, "Yes daddy I will get you some more, I will get you some more." I grabbed her hair and made her face me and rammed my tongue down her throat to make her lose her breath while fucking her from behind. After a good thirty minutes of me sucking and licking pussy and a good 60 minutes of hard-core fucking. I was ready to shoot this nut out my dick! "Turn around bitch, turn around so I can bust this cum all over your face." She turned around with her face to my dick like let me have it daddy. I stroked my "facial juice" all over her face. While she still moaned and stuck her tongue out moving it around, I smeared my juice over her face with the tip of my dick being extra nasty like I was figure painting. I helped her off her knees and lead her toward the shower. She followed in unison wondering how I knew how to please a woman with such satisfaction. I showered up and was ready to go. I went to my stash to make sure everything was on point, and like always it was. I grabbed five more G bundles to give Dave-baby when I'll see him later.

10

CHAPTER

❖

A PROPOSAL

I got into my car the cellphone rang from an unidentified number. I answered saying "Speak" and a voice said, "Big Dawg, this is Dee Are you busy?" I was thinking like *dam he already out of dope.* "Naw lil homie what's up with you are you OK?" Dee replied "I'm cool, I'm cool. I just want to know if me and you could do business without that two faced nigga Spark in our mix?" I said, "Dam baby boy that is going to be kind of hard, me dealing with you and not Spark, we are partners in crime." "Big Dawg" Dee said, "I wouldn't cross you and him up like that I got another block that's cranking with dope fiends forever. I just don't know where else I can get some good dope like you be giving to Dave-baby to serve them." "I know you have better dope than Spark, cause the knocks always tell me." Sounds like you have a business proposition for me Dee I'm listening," I said. "Well, he said I hate to be disloyal to Spark but that nigga only paying me two hundred dollars a day, plus I was waiting on the chance to get back at his ass for how he whooped my ass with that Desert Eagle that night. I'm still gone be coming to the block on the East where y'all at to make it seem like I'm only getting money with Spark and not with you." So, it won't be no problem do you think you can start giving me double ups for whatever money I have?" he asked. "I don't know Dee," I said. Spark has been my partner for 10 years and I don't want to step on his shoes." Dee answered sharply, "Spark don't give a shit about you big brah and I'm not just saying that because I want to do business with you on the side." He said, "I'm telling you because real recognize real and that nigga even said he wanted to kill you." When I heard Dee say that to me, I was devastated. I didn't want to believe him, but something told me he was telling the truth. I said, "You know what Dee for some strange reason I believe what you are saying because my older brother always telling me to dot my

I's and cross my t's when I'm fuckin with him. You are his partner, and I don't think you have no reason to lie." Dee said, "So can we do business big brah?" I said, "Dee I'm gone fuck with you because I got love for you and respect." "When somebody try to accomplish something for themselves to get further and not because of what you just told me, is alright with me" I said. "Cool!" Dee said. I replied, "How much change you working with right now?" Dee responded, "I get two thousand five hundred of Spark's money when you give me the double-up for this. I will be able to give Spark his money back and act like I'm broke." I thought about it and decided to go ahead with the plan. As I backed into Kay-Kay's house to get ten more one-thousand-dollar G bundles, I came back outside and jumped into my car and headed to West Oakland on 35th Ave. I hooked up with Dee, and it was about that time to take a nap and be well rested for later when Spark and I went to the club. It was about six in the evening, and it had been a hectic day for me. I pulled my Nova in the garage my zombie looking second oldest big brother came from the basement in the same rags and that same smell. He said, "Big Dawg let me get another fifty rock on credit until I hit this lick later on tonight." I said, "Nigga you still owe me from the fifty rock I gave you earlier, you said you was gonna pay me today and the day is almost over with." He said, "Big Dawg I'm gonna pay you your money. I just met this little dick sucking toss up and I wanted her to suck me up!" "Man here" I said being a push over for the second time. He turned around and went back into the basement and closed the door without saying thank you as usual. I walked into the house and looked in the oven to see if moms had left the breakfast food for me to eat, but to my surprise it was nothing there but an empty plate with the same crumbs on it. I wanted to ask moms who ate my fucking plate but didn't want to bother her because she had her bedroom door closed. So, I knocked on my oldest big bruh's door to see if he knew who ate my food but didn't get a response. I just said fuck it and ordered a pizza and got rested up for the club later on tonight.

11
CHAPTER
❖
THE SHIT

Adope fiend told me some info about what went down on the block when I wasn't there. He was six one, dirty, stinking, no teeth, and he looked like a walking sardine. He might've been sixty years old; you know one of them Vietnam vets. Sparks grimy ass friends from around the corner rolled up saying, "Ay Spark what's up?" he answered, "Nothing man just trying to figure out where this little bitch ass nigga Dee is at." The grimy friends asked, "Spark we need somebody we can rob so we can kick this heroin sickness we got, you have anybody in mind?" they asked. It was three of them and they were about five four, five nine and five eleven. Their clothes were filthy like they have been dumpster diving or collecting cans. They had scruffy facial hair, hella black and they reminded me of the black crows form The Wiz. Spark answered, "Naw not nobody off hand." The dope fiend overheard him say, "As a matter of fact I do have somebody y'all can rob, y'all know that nigga that I'm in business with?" The grimy friends said, "Yeah, yeah, we know who you talking about, that's the dude in that candy green Nova." Spark said, "Yeah man that's the one, we gone be going to club Ritz later on tonight." He said. "Y'all niggas be outside waiting, when the club ends then y'all run up on his ass by the car then y'all can do whatever you want to him." One of his friends asked, "I thought that was yo patna?" Spark replied, "That nigga ain't nowhere near my patna, I just be acting like we cool until I find the perfect opportunity to take his ass out!" Spark threw one of his homies that was closest to the passenger door a bundle from my stash! It was some of the G bundles that he stole from Dee earlier in the day. The grimy patnas said, "Ay Spark, this is way more to cure our sicknesses." He working with more than this" Spark replied. "I know that nigga will have at least five g's on him plus that big ass chain and medallion piece on. So y'all will have a cool ten G lick off him." "Alright cool" said the grimy homies, "We will be at the Ritz when it's over to strip that nigga to his bare ass." And they drove off laughing. Spark slumped in his bucket ass Monte Carlo and drove off the block looking for his worker Dee. Kay-Kay decided to clean up her house after she and I finished fucking. She went to the grocery store before Boo came back by her house and noticed she hadn't gone yet. He didn't notice when he came to have sex with her because his mind was set on some pussy. But she knew he would notice when he came back, and it wasn't any groceries in the house. She told me she left her house then got in traffic and was thinking about our marathon fucking. She saw a dude in a beat-up ass Monte Carlo blowing his horn at her. She not wanting to stop, because it could've been anybody, she had given her fake number to. Kay-Kay started to speed up a bit and although she dodged the Monte-Carlo in traffic. She made it to the grocery store to buy her groceries and was in the cashier's line to pay for the food. By this time Spark had made it seem like he wasn't following her and appeared in the same line she was in right behind her. When she got ready to pay for her three-hundred-dollar grocery bill, Spark stepped in and said, "Don't worry about that ma, I'll pay for it, I got you." She said, "Thank you, aren't you a nice guy" trying to remember where she recognized him from. Spark said, "It's all good baby there's plenty more where that came from." Okay that's what's up". She said with the look as if she got her another trick ass friend to pay her for companionship. Then she said, "Can you help me put these groceries in the car Mr. there's more were that comes from?" Spark obliged and put every bag in her car while she sat there watching trying to remember where she knew him from. Spark said, "Is it cool if a brutha could help you put those groceries in the house?" He was being messy thinking she already knew he was my 'hommie' from the block. "I don't think that's a good idea, I don't even know your name, nor do you know mines" said Kay-Kay. Spark replied, "I thought you knew who I was, I remember when you were on the block earlier with that "busta" ass nigga Big Dawg?" Then it hit her where she remembers him from and said, "That's where I saw you before, you that nigga that was in the cut looking at me blowing me a kiss with a confused look on her face." He said, "Yeah that's me baby so what do you say how bout we put them groceries up before all your food spoils?" he said. She said, "I know now it definitely ain't no good idea, ain't you and Big Dawg patnas?" He answered and said, "Fuck that fake ass nigga he ain't hardly a friend of mines" she said; "You might have had a better chance to fuck with me if I wouldn't had known you were my man's friend." Now that I know that, I wouldn't even let you smell my body I don't go against the grain baby." She moved him out the way and settled in her car and said, "Thanks for buying me these groceries Mr. there's more where that came from." She told me she started her car and left Spark standing in the parking lot huffing and puffing with a stern rigid look on his face. Soon as she got home and finished putting her groceries away. She called her favorite man to let me know that Spark ain't the real homie. I said, "You know what? You are the second person today who told me this shit I'm gonna have to be careful around that dude because I smell betrayal." I was getting agitated from standing around and said, "We supposed to be going to Club Ritz tonight and I'm going to confront his ass about that shit and see what he has to say!" She said, "Well baby be careful, and I wish you would quit fuckin with him like that." Trying not to go off on her, I changed the subject. "Are you going to be up tonight?" I asked. "Yes, baby yes, baby I will be up tonight" she said thinking I would come by after the club to give her some more of this love potion. I said, "Well good I might need you to serve some of my late-night clientele, so I don't lose any customers. Make sure you answer your phone when I call you." She agreed to serve my customers late night specially when I said we can do another marathon fuckin. I got ready to get in my car to go to the block to catch up with 'Judas' ass Spark. As soon as I got into the car, my second oldest big brother came from the basement saying, "Let me get a fifty rock until I hit this lick tomorrow." My response was, "Bruh you know I can't just keep giving you fifty rocks and you never pay me my money." He said, "lil bro I promise to pay you tomorrow I was just too high to do it." Man, I reluctantly broke my brother off another fifty rocks of crack then he turned around and went into the basement and shut the door…again. Its comical to me so, I just looked at him the whole way and chuckled to myself as I got into the car to find Spark. I arrived on the spot, Spark was standing on Dave-baby's porch counting a big wade of money and said, "Big Bruh where you been the turf was cranking? I done made about ten G's since you were gone." I wanted to bust Spark's ass out about the things I had heard but decided it was not a good time. "Are you ready to hit the club big timer?" I asked. "Yeah, I'm ready" he answered. "Aren't you gone put on some slacks and a shirt or something?" I said. "What's wrong with what I got on?" said Spark. I responded "You've been wearing that shit since we left the mall today and I know you put on a different fit but, I know you ain't washed your ass yet since you shit on yourself. Spark said, "Ay man I'm going just as I am I ain't trying to impress nobody." Then we got into the Nova and drove to the Ritz Club. When we arrived at the club it was packed with bitches everywhere! I was dressed to the nines and even enjoyed being the center of attention because I was dressed to impress and popping bottles of Moet every thirty minutes. Spark just sat at the table and watched me work and get at some of these broads. The club was about to let out and we were already walking toward the door with money on our minds. When we opened the door to come out the club, Spark saw his grimy friends from earlier that were supposed to rob me and said, "Go ahead to the car I got to go and use the bathroom." I was like alright and walked to my car doing a little bit of parking lot pimping. While I walked to my car, three suspicious men I noticed were walking behind me, so I started walking a little faster. One of the grimy dudes said, "A my man, do you have the time?" I said, "Naw brutha I don't have the time." Suddenly one of Sparks grimy friends said, "What's yo name?" then I stopped and turned around to see who these dudes were because, they seem to know who I was. I was thinking here comes the shit. And right when I turned around one of the dudes busted me across my head with the butt of a three fifty-seven revolver. I saw a flash of light as I fell to the ground. I grabbed my forehead to try and stop the bleeding from gushing into my eye. The blood was running down into my eye, and I couldn't see. Now I know what boxers be going through when they are momentarily blinded by their own blood in their eyes. I managed to see the three fifty-seven-revolver pointed at me and I said "Fuck" hella loud trying to see if I even recognized their faces. I didn't know that it was Sparks grimy friends telling me, "Nigga break yo self before we leave yo ass dead where you lay! I had no choice, so I went into my pockets and turned them inside out like rabbit ears. I handed the robbers a load of bills and said that's all I got, and the robbers started jumping me with the three fifty seven again and said, "Nigga that ain't all you got, gimme that chain off your neck." I gave up my chain and anything else that they wanted because I was in survival mode. I wanted to live to fight another day…so to speak. The robbers made me walk the opposite way and told me not to turn around. I did what they said and Spark grimy patnas ran in the other direction letting off three powerful shots of the three fifty seven they used to Jack me with, but they shot it up in the air. I fell to the ground thinking that I was shot but realized I wasn't, and thanked God that Spark's grimy patnas didn't kill me. Suddenly Spark came from nowhere saying, "Dam dawg what happened?" faking like he didn't know what happened to me. I yelled to him, "I just got jacked by some dope fiends who looked like they were about to kill my ass." Spark asked, "You alright?" I said, "Yeah I'm cool I'm just happy they didn't kill me." After I recuperated from the situation I said, "Let's get the fuck out of here before them crazy ass niggas come back. Right at that time my cellphone started ringing. I noticed it was one of my late-night customers and decided I wasn't going to serve anybody until tomorrow night. Too much has already happened to me in one day. I sent them to the voice mail and called Kay-KAY and told her what happened and not to worry about handling my business for tonight. I said that I would see her tomorrow. Kay-Kay was scared for me naturally but was happy I was going home and was safe. She was glad I didn't have her serving anybody because Boo had come back over and was asleep on the couch. She didn't want Boo at her house by himself because he may start going through her belongings and find a brother's stash and wouldn't know how to react. Spark and I ride back to the hood was quiet, but you could feel the tension between the both of us. When we arrived back on the block, he thanked me for the night out on the town and slammed my door. I looked at him as he walked away from my car. I noticed he had an oblivious attitude about what had just happened to me tonight. This time there was no shitting of his pants or scared looks. He was quite stern and like meh. Right when

I was about to confront Spark about what Dee and Kay-Kay told me, Dave-baby was walking toward me and calling my name. Dave-baby says, "I gots to holla at you about something." Somebody stole that last five G bundles you gave me, and I don't know who stole it." Dave-baby was scared thinking that I was going to beat his ass. Instead, I looked at the little homie and said, "That's part of the game," while I showed no anger or hostility toward him. Dave-baby is so loyal, he offered me the five hundred dollars he had earned earlier, and I refused to except it. I gave him another five G bundle and told him to be more careful and to change his stash spot. Dave-baby looked at me we slapped hands and out of nowhere gave me a hug not noticing the gash on my forehead. He told me he wouldn't let me down again and got out the car. I had to take a piss at Dave-baby's house. When I reached the porch his sister Ivory whom I had given the twenty dollars to get her hands and feet done a day ago, was sitting in a chair looking spaced out gritting her teeth. She was rocking back and forth and asked me if I had some weed. I turned around and looked at her and said, "Girl it don't look like you need no weed, you are high as fuck!" Then she said, "I'm off one of those "E pills" I'm on like shit." I know now that my twenty dollars didn't go to a nail shop, it went to the dam 'Ecstasy Man.' Shaking my head and looking at her like really? I gave her some weed to calm her ass down. After that I proceeded to walk into the house because I had to take a piss like a racehorse! Dave-baby's grandmother who was cooking the Cajun fried fish and drinking the Tonka Gin in the kitchen while playing music. She was cussing out everybody in the house saying, "Fuck Ivory that nasty dirty ass bitch ain't nothing but a hoe and fuck El-boogey, that bitch is going to die with a pipe in her mouth, and fuck Dave-baby, because he is a no-good dope selling bastard, and fuck Spark cause that muthafucka sits in front of my house and sells his dope and don't break a bitch off shit! Fuck my hubby Mr. Lock cause that dirty old bastard don't do shit but spend his Social Security check on them crack hoes on the corner." As I walked into the kitchen she said, "Ay man and fuck you too, I don't know what to say about you but muthafucka you done something a bitch don't like, and where's that muthafucka Dee?" She kept on and on while walking to her room to get started on her fifty-piece rock that I gave her earlier that day. Finally, I side stepped her wrath and took a piss and hurried back out the door. I noticed Dee talking to Spark, so I kept it pushing. Everything must have been cool because Spark was smiling and shit. I hopped into my car and proceeded to go home.

12
CHAPTER
❖
MY FIRST HORSE ON THE TRACK

The next day I woke up with a stomachache and ran to the bathroom to worship the porcelain God. I told himself that I was never going to drink so much Moet like that again.

It poured out of my nose and mouth like one of those fish statues in Vegas. The shit burned my nostrils as it was coming out too. When I finished throwing up, I looked at myself in the mirror to observe the gash on my forehead from when I got robbed and pistol whipped. It was a small gash barely noticeable and maybe that was the reason no one seemed to notice it, but hell I sure felt it still. I was so exhausted from last night I had fallen asleep with my casual clothes on that I wore to the club. This fit was one of my favorites and I wanted to take the outfit to the cleaners to see if they could get the blood stains out of the shirt and pants. I jumped into the shower trying to wash off the night from hell that I had from last night. As I got out of the shower and dried off, I had a strange feeling. Suddenly it felt a little bit too quiet and made a brother feel all lonely and shit. Noticing the house was quiet I wondered where everyone was at. I went through the hallway into the kitchen and saw a note on the refrigerator from moms. It read, "Be back went to beauty parlor." I went down the hall and knocked on my oldest brother door and no answer. I was like okay cool I'll just check on my second oldest brother in the basement. I knocked on the door for my brother to 'open up' and he didn't respond. So, I took the liberty of opening it my dam self. Hell, I don't know what is going on in there. When I walked inside, I see him laid out in his clothes with some broads I ain't never seen before snoring up a storm. I backed out quietly not wanting to wake his ass up because I know that he would wake up wanting more credit. At times like this, I wished my father was around, but pops and moms had gotten divorced 6 years ago. My father didn't want anything to do with me since

I was a dope dealer in these East Oakland streets. With the house to myself, I took the opportunity to take my clothes off and roll me a phat blunt and walk around the house naked. After chilling around the house, I decided to get dressed and give J.J. a call. That was the girl that I met at the nail shop yesterday. I grabbed her phone number out of my sweatsuit pocket and dialed her up. A voice answered like they were a gate keeper and said, "Hello" then I said, "Yeah wats up may I speak to J.J.?" The phone dropped like the person who answered the phone was upset because the phone wasn't for them. J.J. came to the phone saying "Hello" in a sarcastic tone like not wanting to be bothered. "What's up baby this is 'Big Dawg' did I catch you at a bad time?" J.J.'s tone of voice came to life like popping popcorn, "Hi Big Dawg! I thought you were one of those 'Bug a Boo's.' Some dudes that's always calling me and don't never be talking about nothing it's about time you called me. The first thought that came to my mind was, "Bitch you da one dat keeps giving yo number out." Anyway, she said, I've been waiting in the house for you to call since I met you yesterday at the nail shop, what's up?" I said, "I thought maybe we could get together and see what you can do with what yo mama gave ya." J.J. answered, "See that's music to my ears baby I need a pimp like you to get me motivated to get some money, my last pimp didn't want to do nothing but eat drink and get his dick sucked all dam day." With the way she was sounding with no shame in her game and so blunt about what she does for a living, made me feel kind of uncomfortable. Truth be told, she was the first actual real hoe I really fucked with, but I wasn't about to show her that. This is going to be my first horse to walk the track. I was going to go with the flow like I was true to it and not new to it. I said, "Do you have those three thousand dollars you said you had for me yesterday?" J.J. said, "Yeah I got it plus I'm ready to make you three thousand more." I said to J.J., "You mean like thirty thousand more, don't you?" I remembered what my older brother told me about not being satisfied with what they give you. She was smiling on the other end of the phone when I said that, and I repeated it again for her to get what I was putting down. She said, "When are you coming to pick me up?" I responded with, "I will be there in about an hour so, hurry up and put your hoe gear on and get ready to do some serious hoeing." She agreed and hung up the phone to get ready to hit the track.

13

CHAPTER

❖

A BEATING FOR ME

I got in my candy green Nova and headed over to Kay-Kay's house to check on my stash. She is hella faithful to me and she keeps my drugs and money at her crib. I don't have to worry about her skipping town because we just like that. I arrived at Kay-Kay's house, and I looked around for Boo's truck and noticed it was nowhere in sight. I exit my Nova, cautiously looking over my shoulder, and used the keys to get into her house. To my surprise she was in her bedroom crying with her head in her lap. I said, "Hey pretty lady what are you crying for?" When she looked up at me, I noticed she had a black eye and a busted lip. I asked, "who did this to you?" She noticed the anger in my voice. She started crying even more not wanting her favorite man to see her like this. She said, "Boo did it baby, but he didn't mean to." I erupted, "You a dam lie, he did mean it if he beat your ass. He definitely meant that shit, how long has he been treating you like this?" Wiping away the tears from her cheeks, "It doesn't happen all the time only when he is stressing about his job," she said. "That don't give a man no right to put his hands on a woman because of some fuckin job, where is that coward ass nigga I'm gonna see if he can hit a man like the way he hit you!" I spoke. Kay-Kay said, "No daddy, no daddy its O.K. please don't do anything to him if you do, I won't be getting my rent and bills paid. I need him daddy because of that. I can take a few bumps and scars for all the money he gives me." I looked at her and knew she was a victim of circumstances… for money. I gave her a smooth pep talk and said, "People living in this lifestyle would get shot, stabbed, or robbed. Some would go to jail, or be crippled, but they would still strive for that all mighty dollar. To do that, you have to have your mind right." Shaking her head in agreement she said, "Alright baby, alright baby I understand." I went to my stash and noticed that I had only a few bundles left and would have to cook up that other kilo of cocaine soon. I told her that I would give her a few thousand to go shopping with to make her feel better. She never mentioned the gash on my head because it was unnoticeable, I guess. I gave her a kiss and told her that I would be back later to check on her. I got in my car and called J.J. to get the directions to her house and told her that I would be there shortly. When I got to the stop sign, Boo was passing by in his truck. The fat fucker slowed down to look at my candy green Nova and noticed it was me driving down their street. He just stared at me, and if looks could kill…

14
CHAPTER
❖
ON YOUR MARK, GET SET, PIMP!

I picked up J.J. and got dam she was looking the part of a hoe ready to get me my money. She had a long fake ponytail sewed in her hair, with some high heel stilettos, and a skirt with a tank top showing her big titties and cleavage. She had big juicy Lucious lips, and an ass like them chicks in Brazil. When she got into the car, she was fascinated to be in the presence of me of course, and she instantly handed me the three thousand dollars she had for me. I didn't count it and barley looked at it then put it in my pocket. I never experienced doing any real pimping, I just used to talk pimping with my brothers. The game was starting to make me nervous, but I wouldn't let it show. I said, "Baby check this out, you are going to have to show me that you are serious about being with me. I'm going to give you a 90-day trial to prove your loyalty, us pimps call a new hoe being down with us prospect hoes, after that you will be a full member of my stable." J.J. said, "O.K. Big daddy I will do as you say like a good hoe and pay you all of my money and walk that track until my heels bleed to make you happy." I 'dug' what J.J. was saying to me and showing her dedication to become my permanent hoe. I said, "First I'm gone start you off on E 14th by High Street to see how you do on that track, if you do good then I will take you to another track aite?" J.J. replied, "Yes daddy" like she was in a trance and hanging on my every word. I could see that she was getting up for this shit too. It must've been exciting for her as well. You gotta be built different to do something like this. When we arrived on our new location or the track if you will. I told her a time and designated place where I would meet her. I also told her that I would be watching her to make sure she was safe. J.J. got out the car and immediately started waving and blowing kisses to car's driving by like a boss. She was 'in it to win it' and she displayed the perfect attitude. I wondered why this bitch didn't have a cellphone and figured I guess that's why hoe's need pimps, because they are too naive to think of the smallest things to help them with their hoeing. As I parked, I thought about something positive that I could invest my illegal earned money into. I produced the idea of a trucking company. I always loved to drive and figured driving one of those big rig trucks would be fun. So now I had a new goal and that was to start my own trucking company. I still had some bags of weed left and rolled me up another blunt while I waited on J.J. to come back with the money she had made on the track. After about 2 hours of sitting in the car thinking she finally came back. She looked like hell had hit her across the face, but I knew it was just her working the streets with the tricks. J.J. said, "I got one thousand five hundred dollars right now daddy, plus I stole a chain and watch from this trick when he fell asleep." I took the money and observed the chain like a jeweler would at his store. The watch was hella clean it was a Rolex Presidential and the chain was a Versace link. "Dam" I said, "I only been with you for 2 hours, and I got fifteen hundred and some jewelry. I can see us going to the top quick baby as long as we got each other." J.J. started blushing and said, "You want me to get back out there and get you some more money daddy?" I said, "Baby daddy has to make a few stops before we can get back out there and play." I started my car, cracked the window open because ole girl was ripe. We drove to the hood. When I got to the block Dave-baby was the first to greet me. He said, "Here goes your five G's big brah" and when J.J. seen that her eyes jumped out her sockets! She kept quiet and stayed out a pimp's business like a good hoe should. I gave Dave-baby his five hundred dollars and five more G bundles. He darted off not wanting to be dirty in case the rollers hit the block. Dave-baby in my eyes was the epitome of being hungry and trying to hustle to get it all. I saw Spark on Dave-baby's porch counting a gang of cash in the open then he hid it under Dave-baby's porch. He came out to say What's up to his friend. "What it do?" I startled Spark. I felt that now was the time to confront this boy about things he said about me. Looking antsy J.J. said, "Daddy I can go up on the corner and make my money while you are on the block, I will run circles around them crack hoes up there." I looked at her for a hot second, and then gave her permission to do it. Spark was watching and getting more jealous of me. J.J. got out the car and Spark looked like he even wanted to spend a few dollars on that pussy. "Dam Big Dawg you wasn't playing about that pimp shit, was you?" I didn't respond to that back hand compliment, but I told him to get in the car. I took the liberty of getting myself together before I tore into his ass and said, "Man Spark I thought we was patnas." Spark said, "Man what the fuck you talking about?" I said, "I heard you tried to holla at my broad Kay-Kay when she was at the grocery store and then you had the audacity to tell her I wasn't a friend of yours and fuck me." Spark had a look of disbelief on his face and said "Ay bruh I would never say no shit like that." I did get at this broad at the grocery store, but I didn't know it was your broad. You are my best friend, and I would never cross your back like that." I'm trying my best not to sock this dude in his mouth, and I started to tell him what Dee said but I didn't want to get him in trouble with Spark. I started to get agitated and said, "Man after all the shit I have done for you out here, how you gone stab me in the back like that?" He answered, "You gone believe a bitch over yo patna?" Then I had to pump my brakes for a minute and thought about it. "I guess you right dog." Looking relieved Spark said, "People want to see our friendship crumble they want to see me, and you fall out behind some he say she say shit. You are sharper than that, stay focused and fuck those people trying to divide and conquer us." With that said I believed my patna Spark. I calmed down a bit and said, "Don't even trip maybe it's the gash in my head that's got my mind playing tricks on me." We shook hands and got out the car. As a piece offering, I asked him if he wanted to smoke and he said, "Fire it up!" I went back to my car and grabbed a few philly blunts and a bag of weed I had from the weed spot. When I grabbed the weed, I saw a business card sitting on the passenger car seat where Spark was sitting. I read the business card and it was from a detective for the police department. I was in disbelief and said to Spark, "Say bruh is this your card?" He said, "Oh yeah that's the card that the "po.po." gave me about a robbery that happened in the neighborhood… he lied. Now my curiosity has peeked, and I said, "Why is Task Force interested in a robbery, and why would they ask you of all people?" He responded, "Um, uh maybe cause they know I'm always out here." I was not inquiring the questions to Spark as if he was a snitch, I was just asking on 'GP' general principal. Then a dope fiend came and approached us asking for some crack for five dollars. I wasn't tripping and was about to serve him when Spark intervened and told the dope fiend to go by and stand on Dave-baby's porch where he had stashed his money. I told him, "Spark you need to slow down on being so quick to serve people." He responded, "Man you know how I am when it comes to this money." The dope fiend waited to get his crack, and Spark came to serve him. Spark said, "Man these dope fiends are crazy as hell, did you see the way that muthafucka walked away?" I replied, "Them dope fiends is sharp they ain't as stupid as we think they are." J.J. walked back to me from the corner of my place of business 'the block.' She was getting her prostitution on and said, "Daddy are you finished handling your business, because its slow over here and tricks want, they dick's sucked for ten dollars and I charge three hundred for thirty minutes? I said, "Yeah baby I'm just about done here, let's go back to Hight Street and see what we can come up with." Spark was looking at me now that I think about it with more jealousy and envy than ever. He wished he could've had a woman as pretty as mine, let alone to hoe for him. When we got in the car to go to the 'track' on High St. she said, "Daddy did you see the way your boy was looking at you when I walked up wanting to go?" I said, "Naw baby I didn't notice why?" "Well, he looked like he was straight hating on you because you have me hoeing for you." I answered, "That's my boy he ain't got no reason to be jealous of me he got way more paper than

I do." She said, "Daddy don't you know people will hate on you because you are a natural born player and have characteristics that money can't buy?" I took that in for a minute and then answered, "Baby why would anybody hate on me because I'm a natural born player, anybody can be a player in the game." She knew when I said that I wasn't the big pimp she thought I was. I guess that was better for her, because now she can make me the pimp that she wanted me to be. Then she said with sincereness in her face, "Daddy, I don't want you touching drugs ever again, after my 90-day prospect hoe time is up I don't want you to do nothing but rest, dress, and finesse and let me do the rest." I liked the sound of that, so I agreed to try that because I was just thinking about how I didn't want to touch drugs any more anyway. We drove to the track with nothing but money on our minds.

15
CHAPTER
❖
THE ATROCITY

Meanwhile Spark stood on the block serving the knocks as usual. When his pockets were stuffed to capacity with money, he went to Dave-baby's house to put the money he just made, with the money he already stashed under the porch. He reached under the steps and to his surprise his money was gone! He started getting angrier by the minute thinking of who could have stolen his money. One of the little homies told me how Spark flashed on everybody after I left the block. Me and my hoe stayed by the car just chilling so it wasn't us. Dee hadn't come through since last night, but Dave-baby got a fresh bundle from me when I pulled up and ran in the house. So that meant in Spark's mind that it had to be Dave-baby or somebody in his family who the porch belonged to. Spark immediately grabbed his gun and put it under his waist then ran up the porch and kicked in Dave-baby front door. Once inside the house he walked up to the first person he saw and that was El-boogey Dave-baby's mother. He hit her in the eyes demanding to know where his money was. Dave-baby grandmother came out of her room hearing the commotion and Spark turned and slapped grandmother in the face. The slap was so powerful and quick it made her mouth split and blood started spilling out. Ivory came from the living room yelling at him for his actions and he kicked her in her stomach making her fall to her knees. Suddenly Dave-baby appeared from the dining room and swung at Spark with a closed fist. He missed and Spark pulled out his Desert Eagle pistol- and pistol-whipped him to a bloody pulp. All the while he was thinking *maybe Dave-baby stole my money because I stole his bundle that big dawg had given him yesterday.* He knew Mr. Lock didn't do it because he already has money. Then Spark started doing destructive shit by shooting at the roof, the TV, refrigerator, stove, and any other things he could shoot at. After his rampage on the family, he stormed out the house, mad as hell.

16
CHAPTER
❖
ANOTHER ASS KICKING

The nosey neighborhood old lady flagged me down one day and told me about Kay-Kay getting beat up by her boyfriend. She said Kay-Kay was screaming and crying till she ran out of breath saying, "No baby, no baby, please don't hit me anymore Big Dawg came to my house unexpectedly I didn't know he would come by. I can't help it if he knows where I live, I'm sorry, I'm so sorry!" Boo replied as he was whooping her with a hanger, "You lying ass bitch, I told you not to be fuckin with that punk ass nigga. I saw that nigga in his green Nova at the stop sign right on your block talking on his cellphone writing down something on some paper." Boo continued to whip and beat her until blood and welts appeared on her red bone complexion. When he paused to get his wind back, she pleaded with him and said, "Baby I love you why do you think I would fuck back with him? Do you think if I didn't love you I would except this kind of abuse from you?" He hesitated before striking her again without the slightest thought that she was only messing with him because he paid her bills. I guess the gruesome truth was that he was in love with her, but she was not in love with him. He said, "Baby I'm sorry, I don't know what's gotten into me lately. I just love you so much. The thought of another man touching you makes me want to do something to somebody. Please Kay-Kay don't make me kill you behind my jealousy that I have over you. If you don't really like me or don't want to be with me, then tell me now and I will except it like a man." She got scared of what he just said but, the money he was giving her for her bills was still worth playing with his emotions. She said, "Baby I want you for the rest of my life, and you don't have to worry about Big Dawg, or any other man till we both are dead and gone…" she lied. He fell to the couch and started sobbing with bubbles of snot coming out his nose saying how sorry he was for beating on her and for not trusting her. To make it up to her, he would go to the bank on Monday and give her some money out of his savings account. Kay-Kay tears stopped, and she started rubbing his back and asked, "How much money are you going to give me?" She was thinking this probably was the best time especially after he gave her a black eye and whipped her like a stepchild. Boo said, "How much do you need?" and she replied five thousand dollars baby" with a wicked smirk. He said, "No problem baby I will have it for you on Monday." After she got up from the couch in disgust on how much of a sucker he was. She would head to the bathroom to access the damage. Instantly she would think of nothing more than to hustle and give me all and anything that I desired. She would take a thousand ass whippings from Boo to give the money to her favorite man…me.

17
CHAPTER

❖

THE INDECENT PROPOSAL

J.J. and I pulled into the auto parts store parking lot to meet with the homie, Dee. He was there waiting standing near a phone booth. He sees me roll up and he gets into my car and handed me the four G's for the double-up action. I gave him five G's for his services. Dee said, "Big-brah I'm not ever coming back to the block. I gots to get it out here in West Oakland man. I don't have to answer to nobody or don't have to worry about coming up short on Spark's money. I hope me, and you can still be down to do business." I shook my head up and down in an agreeing way and said, "For show Dee I understand how you feel, it comes a time when a man has to bounce and carry his own weight. Just don't forget about me when you blow up and become rich." I willingly gave Dee his five thousand dollars' worth of G bundles for the four thousand I had given him. I gave him a handshake hug and told him to call me if he needed anything ever. Dee told me to do the same and that he would always be my little brah. He got out of my car and headed to the direction of his million-dollar block. I was running low on product and would have to cook up that other kilo I had, but I'll worry about that later. I had some more pimping to do and the money was calling me. J.J. and I went back to the track so that she could serve some more tricks. This time I didn't sit in the car and wait. I walked around and observed the track for the first time in my life and couldn't believe the things I was seeing. Ole girly was excited about me being out on the track with her. This was show off time, and she could show the other hoe's how sexy her man is. She wanted to let other pimps no that she had a man and not to fuck with her, while she was soliciting her sexual pleasures. I peeped game on the other pimps driving the cleanest cars from Cadillac Escalades, Mercedes Benz, to seven forty-five I BMWs. I felt out of place with my old school Nova while theses fools were shining with their new whips.

I see how some of the pimps were dressed in casual wear like slacks, docker's and linen. They wore things you wear to the club on a regular basis. I felt under dressed really but, I could smell that this new game I entered was a lucrative underworld. I would definitely have some more questions for my oldest brother when I see him at home. J.J. said, "Daddy I'm gonna make the block a few times to try and catch me one of these tricks driving by. I will meet you at the car in about two hours O.K?" I told her to be careful and that I would meet her at the car when she is finished. I was overwhelmed by the pretty young bitches out here getting their man's money. I was also tripping off how the pimps would be trying to talk to the hoes, and they would walk away from then not trying to hear a word they had to say. I stepped inside a coffee shop to sit and think for a minute. I started thinking about going to school to get my class A license so that I could drive one of those big rigs and start a trucking company. I do realize that nobody retires from being 'in the life.' Either they go to prison, or they end up dead. Suddenly, a fire ass stallion walked in and ordered herself some coffee. I was shocked that the girl was as beautiful as she was, and I offered her a chair to sit at my table. The stallion saw how sexy a brother was and accepted my offer then said, "I know I'm not supposed to sit here and talk to you, but you seem to make me comfortable by the look in your eyes. She acted like it was an indecent proposal or something. She unzipped her jacket all sexy and shit and said, my name is Sasha what's yours?" Sasha was six foot one, with a professional dancer's body. Her hair was big, burgundy, and bumped up with some of it hanging wildly in her face. Her eyes were big and sleepy looking with a perfect nose, and thin sexy ass lips. Her facial expression was one of don't fuck with me unless I tell you to. I was tripping to myself why she wasn't supposed to be sitting talking to me and remembered. I was on a hoe track and that hoes ain't supposed to speak to pimps unless they want to choose a new man. I was taking back by that and then I got my thoughts together and said, "Baby they call me Big Dawg, and if you sitting here talking to me and see comfort in my eyes then you must be choosing me today to be your man." Sasha was feeling how I introduced myself like a gentleman and I knew about the rules of the game. She said, "Big Dawg huh?" I like that name I never seen you around here before, you must be new in town, or are you just starting to get your feet wet?" I responded, "What makes you think I'm either new in town or just getting my feet wet?" She replied, "Well, Mr. Man for starters your wearing jeans, a T-shirt, and some sneakers. Pimps don't wear that when they come to the track." I got embarrassed for a little bit but came back strong with, "Bitch you ain't all that to be talking to me like that." She said, "Take it easy, and your cute, but I already have a pimp and I'm happy with him." She said, "I tell you what, there are no hard feelings here, and here is a hundred dollars for your conversation." Then Sasha the stallion gulped her coffee and told me she would see me around and left. I was stunned by the way She just broke me off a hundred dollars like that, and I told myself that I would take this pimp game more serious. My cellphone had rung, and it was Kay-Kay. I Hollered at her about how I found a hoe and that she had already given me a three thousand dollar choosing fee. She also gave me fifteen hundred in 2 hours plus a Versace chain and a Rolex watch. Kay-Kay cheered her "favorite man" on and told me how she would have five Gees for me on Monday from that buster Boo. She knew not to tell me what she went through to get the five Gees because it might upset her "favorite man." She also stated that she was glad I was figuring out other ways to make money besides selling dope. Also, I shared with her about going to put myself through truck driving school to start a trucking company. Kay-Kay said she would do everything to help me, and she would never leave my side. We hung up the phone from each other. I left the coffee shop wanting to know where my 'red-light' wife was at and to make sure she was OK. I looked back and forth but couldn't find her. I decided to surprise her with a cellphone, why not she earned it. I jumped back into my car and road to the nearest tele-communications store and bought J.J. a cellphone. I drove back to the same place where I had parked before and saw my 'red light' wife waiting patiently for her pimp to come back. When she got into the car, she handed me fifteen hundred again and some stolen credit cards. She said with an earnest plea, "Daddy we better hurry up and use these cards before the trick realizes they are stolen and call his Credit Bureau!" As we drove off laughing, I stuffed the money in my pocket and said, "Look what I got for you baby" and handed her a new cellphone. She got all emotional and shit and started to cry and said, "Daddy, nobody has never bought me anything" and hugged her pimp. I said in a reassuring way, "See baby I told you when you start showing me how loyal you are to me, I would give you the world." Then we rode out to the nearest mall to use the stolen credit cards blasting music.

18
CHAPTER

❖

SNITCHING AT ITS FINEST

Back on the block, Spark was still upset about his money coming up missing and he wanted to know where his worker Dee was at. Dee didn't owe Spark anything so he couldn't be mad at him. Spark assumed that Dee didn't want to sell dope anymore and took the money and bounced up out of there. Spark had the block to himself for a while until Dave-baby came outside after getting the shit beat out of him from Spark earlier. Dave-baby stayed and conducted his business on one end of the block while Spark conducted his on the other end. Whenever Dave-baby and I was on the block all the dope fiends would go to us because the dope fiends felt cool around us. We weren't dogging them out like Spark does his clients. Dope fiends didn't buy their crack from Spark because they knew he had too much baking soda in his crack and would only spend with him if we weren't around. So, by Dave-baby being on the other end of the block, all the dope fiends went to where he was. They didn't think twice about spending their money with Spark. This did nothing but make him more furious! It was bad enough thinking Dave-baby, or his family stole his money. Spark had enough and thought of something else he could do to hurt Dave-baby and his family. He wanted to get him robbed but he couldn't think of who could do it right now at this moment. His grimy patnas that robbed me and busted me over the head and put that gash on my forehead was nowhere to be found since that night. They probably went somewhere with the money they got from me and overdosed in some hotel somewhere…I hope. Fuck em there's plenty of more where that came from. Some of the lil homies on the block heard that Spark was going to do something hella shiesty. That fucker called up the Oakland Task Force Division on his cellphone. In passing, some of the homies overheard him on the phone and he said. "Hey detective this is Spark do you remember me?"

Spark said, "Yeah that's me, I was wondering if we can come to a term of negotiations when it comes to getting some drug dealers out of the neighborhood?" Spark said, "All I want in return is for you to look the other way when you and your fellow police officers see me on the block." Spark looked around to see if anybody was listening to him and he answered, "I will give you two drug dealers for right now, one they call Big Dawg, and the other they call Dave-baby. He proceeded to tell them that I was a big fish, and that Dave-baby is a little fish. Both could be caught with a gang of dope on them. He covered up the phone and began looking around like he planned the perfect surprise party. The only thing was we weren't happy to be the guest of honor. Spark put his plan into action immediately and told the detective, "There is a drug dealer that people call him Dave-baby on the opposite corner of where I'm standing. He has rocks in his mouth and has about two thousand dollars on him. If you come now, you can catch him in the act."

19
CHAPTER
❖
THE ROUGH INTRODUCTION

After Spark had beat up Dave-baby and family the other day. They feared him even more so that, neither one of them wanted to call the police out of fear of what he might come back and finish! They waited on me patiently like kids in kindergarten getting ready to receive their treats by that I meant, to bring them their daily dose of crack cocaine. El-boogey was staring out the window looking at her son Dave-baby sell dope to the neighborhood dope fiends. Her face lite up as my hoe and I pulled up to the curb with a whole lot of shopping bags. I said, "Dam Dave-baby look how this pimp game got ya boy stunting out here." He said, "I see big brah" with no malice in his heart, "You look like you done spent about ten thousand in the mall. "I said, "I ain't spent shit not one dime. My lady of leisure came up on some tricks credit cards out of his wallet while he was asleep. So, me and her went shopping before he could wake up and report his credit cards stolen." He replied, "Man big brah you might as well become a full-time pimp, what if you had more than one hoe hoeing for you imagine that?". I said, "I even brought you a couple of pairs of shoes little homie." He had a grateful surprised look on his face as I dug into the back seat of my car and tossed two pairs of Nike Air Force Ones, a white pair, and a black pair to him. He told me, "Thanks big brah I appreciate you!" Right then the Detective and two squad cars rolled up jumping out their vehicles yelling freeze! We put our hands up while J.J. sat in the car. The detective grabbed Dave-baby by his throat and started choking him because he saw that he was trying to hurry up and swallow the rocks he had in his mouth. The detective turned and socked me in my stomach. He snatched J.J. out of my Nova by her wrist twisting her arm and handcuffed all three of us. First, he frisked me, grabbing all on my balls and shit and squeezing them so hard I fell to my knees. He frisked Dave-baby and dug in his pockets and found the two thousand dollars Spark said he had and put it in his pocket. When he got to J.J. he felt on her pussy and titis then ran his fingers between the crack of her ass. The detective said to me proudly, "You must be the big fish they call Big Dawg?" I answered saying "Yeah that's my name, but I ain't no big fish and how did you know my name?" The detective started to laugh and then punched me in the jaw saying, "I ask the questions around here you dope dealing son of a bitch! Now turn your black ass around nigger before I run your ass downtown!" By the way that he had that look in his eyes, *like I really want to beat your ass right now to a pulp,* I had to oblige him. The detective then turned his wrath to Dave-baby and said, "Ah you must be the small fish they call Dave-baby, how do you like working for the big fish?" He continued, "I bet this money belongs to Big Dawg but now it belongs to me. I could use these two thousand dollars to pay off a few bills." Dave-baby trying to think fast on his feet said, "I don't work for dude, my grandmother gave me that money." The detective looked at him like *this nigga got the audacity to try and cover it up* and said, "Shut your fuckin trap you dumb ass nigger bastard or I'll run your ass downtown with his black ass. What do you guys think I don't know what's up?" Now the detective turned his attention to J.J. and said, "My, my, my aren't you a nice thick ugly whore. why don't we make the block in my squad car, and you can put your nice fat juicy black lips around my dick?" She replied, "I'm no whore I work for a living you crooked two-faced greasy pig!" I wouldn't suck a pig's dick with my worst enemy's lips." The detective hauled off and slapped her in her face and said, "You nigger bitches are all the same, always have something smart to say when you need to shut your fuckin mouth." The detective and his unit ran everybody's name through the system, and we all came back clear. Then he said, "I bet not catch you muthafucka's around here again now get your asses off my block before I really get upset." They all got back into their patrol cars looking like cowboys in the olden days with a smirk and drove off without looking twice at Spark down on the other end of the block. When the detective left from jacking us, we all had the look on our faces like dam that was close we could've been gone. Especially after I went on a shopping spree with that trick's credit cards. I didn't know what to expect. J.J. feeling all sentimental and shit, told me this was one of the reasons she didn't want me selling drugs anymore as she sat on my green Nova fixing herself. Dave-baby brought it to my attention that it didn't seem right him how the detective just seems to come straight to us like somebody called. Since Spark's money came up missing from under the porch, and he did the rain dance on the family seemed a little bit suspect. My jawbone and balls were in pain with a constant throbbing but, I was relieved that nobody went to jail and that the detective was gone. Spark came from the other side of the corner and said, "A man are y'all alright?" I said, "We are now where did that racist ass cop come from, he isn't one of the usual cops that come thru the block and keep going, and how did he know me and Dave-baby?"

20
CHAPTER
❖
SORRY NOT SORRY

"**M**an, he probably busted one of these dope fiends in the neighborhood with some crack and a base pipe. They must've told him everything" said Spark trying to convince us. I said "You may be right because how he just road up on me and Dave-baby it was like someone already gave him a heads up on how we do our program. *Spark should've won an academy award for the way he was acting like he didn't know shit.* It kept bugging me how I feel like I had heard or saw the detective's name somewhere before. When Spark heard me mention that, he got nervous as hell and changed the subject saying, "Man guess what? Somebody in Dave-baby house stole my money from under the porch. "I beat the shit out of everybody in that joint. I had to bust Dave upside his head because he was throwing punches at me." Then he said proudly, "I didn't do him like I could have because I know that's your worker." I said, "Spark, the homie just told me you did that shit. You hella wrong for putting your hands on those people like that, and they let you sell all the dope you want too out of their yard. You don't even give them a fucking dime." I told him, "You know just like I know, taken losses is part of the game and you just don't go swinging on our 'business' partners." I was looking at him and thinking *I should just whoop his ass.* But that's when El-boogey the little homies mother yelled for me to come inside the house. I already knew what she wanted, especially after getting beat up by Spark punk ass. So, I told Dave-baby to give me a few fifty rocks out of the three G bundle and that he didn't have to worry about the two thousand dollars that the detective took. He could keep the rest of what was left out of the three G bundle to help him buy his car and apartment. He had a confused look on his face at first but then he gave me the few fifty rocks. I was going to give it to El-boogey when I walked into the house. She met me at the front door looking angry and scared at the same time. Almost as if she was in a car accident that flipped her car over twelve times, and luckily, she made it out alive. She screamed, "That no good nigga came in here beating on me, my mother, my daughter then pistol whipped my son! He started shooting everything in da house!" Dave-baby sister said while taking short breaths, "That muthafucka is crazy somebody needs to do something to his ass before my daddy Mr. Lock kills em!" I answered them with assurance and said, "Don't worry about Spark y'all, he will get his one day because God don't like ugly." El-boogey chimed in and said, "I don't know why he would think we would steal from him; we don't get down like that." She said, "Hell we would rather beg you to death then steal from anybody, it was only one person who was by our porch that I didn't recognize. I think Spark knew him because he served him hella crack." Then I remembered that five dollars knock that Spark was so in a rush to serve. I said, "I will see y'all tomorrow because I got this pimp thing going on, plus I need to cook up some more coke." I'm going to talk to Spark about his attitude for y'all too." They all seemed a little bit better from talking to me. Now I'm on my way to holler at Spark and his bad for business attitude. I said, "Dog guess what I just remembered?" He acting all interested and flabbergasted about what is about to come out of my mouth next. He said, "What's that Big Dawg?" I said, "Do you remember that five dollars knock you told to go and stand by the porch earlier before you served him?" He said, "Yeah I remember." I said, "I bet that's the nigga that stole your money." All of a sudden, his ass had an epiphany and said, "Snapp I bet that muthafucka did and that's why his ass walked off so fast so I wouldn't figure it out!" Spark started feeling ashamed and felt like he had albumen on his face about how he blamed Dave-baby and his family. He all but sucked it up and said, "Fuck it what's done is done, you can't cry over spilled milk" as if his actions weren't wrong. I couldn't believe this brazenness, and ruthlessness, that was coming from this niggas mouth. I had to get at that dude and let him know that he needs to stop jumping to conclusions so fast, and that he needs to change his fucking attitude. Spark tried to downplay how he was wrong and said he would apologize to Dave-baby and his family, but it never happened. Sorry not sorry.

21
CHAPTER
❖
HOW ABOUT NOW?

I left the block after getting jacked by the detective and talking to Spark. J.J. and I went to my house to get a little rest and to put away all the bags we had from going shopping with the stolen credit cards. As we were carrying all the bags from the car into the house, my oldest brother and his bottom bitch T.T. rolled up in this black-on-black Cadillac Fleetwood Brougham. He looked at J.J. and then at me and instantly, game recognized, game! From him being in the pimp game so long he already knew J.J. was a hoe by what she was wearing and that his youngest brother took his advice and started getting his knowledge about the pimp game. My brother and T.T. got out the car and he said, "Well, well, well what do we have here looked like the game God is giving somebody some blessings." I said, "I told you big brah I'm trying to be a factor of this pimp game like you." Big brother said, "All you have to do is really want it and stay down like four flat tires on a broken-down Chevy." We laughed. We both walked into the house with our ladies. I asked my brother could I holler at him after I took J.J. to my room. He said what's on yo mind brah?" I had to gather my thoughts and then I tried not to come off as I didn't know what I was doing. I said, "Ay big bruh, I need to get a little pimp counseling from you." Big Bruh answered, "For show lil brah, let me get this bitch situated in my room and I'll come out and holla at you." We met in the living room after fifteen minutes later I blurted out about five or six questions like rapid fire all at one time. He told me to slow down and take my time, but I just had so many questions. I took a deep breath and asked, "Do I need to call my hoe a bitch all the time?" Big Bruh said, "Well lil brah it all depends on the relationship you and your woman have. All hoes don't like to be addressed as bitches. Some would think that you're calling them a hoe or a bitch because you are upset with them." He said, "For instance T.T. likes for me to call her a bitch or a hoe because she knows I'm feeling "pimpish" when I say it." So, I'm soaking all of this in as if I was the statue of the thinking man. I asked, "Has another pimp ever took one of your hoes before?" Big Bruh responded, "Hell yeah, another pimp has taken one of my hoes before. When things like that happen, it will let you know if this game is for you or are you going to keep pimpin!" He said, "Find you another hoe or tuck your tail between your ass and gain the corner and start pouting." I asked, "How many hoes have you had at one time?" Big Bruh said, "I had up to at least 10 hoes at one time. We pimps call it "100 toes down", but as I grew older in the game, I came to realize you're dealing with 10 problems, 10 personality's, 10 situations, and sometimes the money wasn't adding up right. Keep this in mind, one bad bitch is better than ten. Don't nobody want a busted ass looking hoe, you know somebody who reminds them of their wife. They want the fantasy by fucking with a bad bitch. Someone that they can't always fuck on. Sometimes that one bitch can put more money in your pocket than ten normal looking bitches." I said, "Where is the best place to take your hoe to get some money?" Big Bruh looked intently at me and smiled and said, "Las-Vegas baby, Las Vegas." Hoes get paid up to one thousand dollars an hour and have lesser work to do. As opposed to charging about three to four hundred dollars in most places in this country. You can find other spots for a bitch to get your money like, at big events, business meetings, and shit like that. But lil brah let me tell you, you can sit here and ask me a million questions, but there is nothing that can get you ready for the game but experience." As he leaned back into his chair fingers crossed on the lower part of his belly chilling. As I received the pertinent information into my mental rolodex I said, "O.K big brah I understand basically you are telling me experience is the best way to learn about the pimp game, right?" Big Bruh responded, "Right, but if you ever get stuck between a rock and a hard spot don't hesitate to give your big brother a jingle." For the first time in life Big Bruh handed me, his little brother a cellphone number and told me that he loved me. I can call about any questions I wanted to inquire about as far as the game goes. After that was said and done Big Bruh went to his room to be with T.T. With her fine thick ass. After I digested what was said to me, I stood up and went to my room to be with J.J. as well. I entered the room and J.J. was putting my clothes on hangers and straightening up the room. We smoked a few blunts then laid on the bed to watch a DVD movie. I heard J.J. got up close to me and proceeded to put her arms around my neck. She was looking like she wanted to say something, but she didn't know how to say it. Finally, she said, "I'm serious about not wanting you to sell drugs anymore." I looked at her dead in her face and said, "I don't plan on it, I planned on going to school to get my class A license so I can open a trucking company. I want to make money the legit way. I'm going to find out what its costs to put myself through the Trucking Education Program and get my business license and start from there." J.J. said, "Daddy after my prospecting probation is up with you,

I want you to start calling me bitch, okay?" She was looking all seductive and shit and said, my name won't be J.J. anymore it will be bitch; I can tell that you are new to this but I'm going to make you the best pimp in the world. I'm going to turn you into a monster. You will know all the fundamentals of pimping and you will be the most respected pimp in the game when I'm done with you." At first, I sat there and pondered if I should slap her or fuck the shit out of her. That type of shit turns me on when she came at me like that. I said, "I appreciate what you're doing J.J. putting your time and effort into me like this when you could've fucked with any pimp in Oakland who already knows way more about this pimp shit than me. She just smiled at me with approval, and I told her, "I will always remember you until I turn into dust." Then we laid cuddling each other as we both went fast asleep.

22
CHAPTER

❖

THE BEGINNING OF THE END

After a few months had passed, I peeped how loyal J.J. was and I was able to put myself through Trucking School after all. Thanks to both of my girls handling their business, with that extra five thousand dollars that Kay-Kay gave me I was making progress to get out of the dope game. I was still selling drugs and pimping at the same time. I sold my candy green Nova to Dave-baby and bought myself a new burgundy Ford Expedition. It's an Eddie Bauer edition SUV and I put some T.V.'s in it and some twenty-four-inch true chrome rings on it. I was doing my part to keep up with the rest of the pimps who were driving new cars. The house that Dave-baby had lived in, ended up burning to the ground after the man of the house Mr. Lock passed away. I don't know what happened as to why it caught on fire. Maybe somebody was too high over there and burnt some shit down, I don't know. Kay-Kay and Boo are still together, and she is still seeing me her "favorite man" from time to time. Spark and I still sold our drugs on the block with business as usual. Dave-baby was still my partner and Dee still bought his dope from me and sold his drugs in West Oakland. El-boogey, and Ivory still came through the block every now and then even though they lived in a homeless shelter. The detective and Spark were still helping each other out. I had to bounce and get my own space, so I got an apartment. My brother still stayed at home and retreated to the basement. I had coped an apartment in the Hayward Hills near Cal State Hayward College. The apartment had three swimming pools, a fitness center with a full-length basketball court, tennis courts and a recreation center big enough to throw a high school Senior Ball there. Life was good, and I decided to take Kay-Kay to San Francisco to a high price restaurant. We were stuffing our faces with crab noodles, oysters, shrimp, mussels, and champagne. I thought about my investment and decided to give J.J. a call.

She was on the track working hard for me, so I decided to give her a call. I dialed her number and she picked up quickly and said, "Hey daddy what's up?" I responded, "Bitch what's up with you?" She said, "Nothing much daddy just suckin a tricks dick to get you your money, what are you doing?" I said, "Aww bitch I'm not doing too much just stuffing my face with some good food over in Frisco, I just wanted to call and check in on you to see what you were up to. Get back to suckin and fuckin for me and I will call you later." She said, "O.K. Daddy, I should have about thirty-five hundred dollars for you when I see you." She hung up the phone like she was planning a surprise party for me. As I finished scarfing down some delicious shrimp I said to Kay-Kay, "Dam this pimp game has been good to me, I'm gonna have to find me another hoe so I can have double what J.J. is paying me." Kay-Kay said, "Daddy I would get down with some tricks for you, but I just don't have the heart to do it like J.J." She looked at me sheepishly and said, "I would rather keep meeting boyfriend tricks to pay you." I wiped the corners of my mouth with my napkin, sat back in my chair and said, "It's still a form of hoeing, it's just on a different dimension, I really ain't tripping as long as it's a profit." I then continued to finish off my mussels, and oysters and enjoyed the ambiance of the restaurant with a glass of wine. Kay-Kay agreed with a head nod and proceeded to finish off her meal. Afterwards I took her back to the house and made my way to the track to see J.J. and to collect the earnings from her. I arrived at the track; I saw this hoe walking that looked familiar to me. I slowed down my Expedition SUV and said, "Hey bitch if you knew better you would do better, come fuck wit me. Let me give you some of this great pimpin that I got." She paused and looked really hard at me for a second. I told her, "Hey bitch, pimpin in your mouth can you taste it?" The familiar beat walker stopped and turned toward me. When I saw who it was I ain't gone lie, I got a few butterflies in my stomach. I gathered my composure like a basketball player getting ready to shoot his two free throws for the game. I said, "Sasha? Bitch what's up? Are you still happy with your pimp or are you ready to come fuck with a real one hundred percent pimp with class?" She recognized me and said, "My pimp is looking at me right now, yell your cell number to me and I will call you when I have the chance." She said it as if, we were in class and passing notes trying not to get busted by the teacher. I was like okay cool, and I yelled out my cell number to her and blasted off in the Ford Expedition S.U.V. J.J. had called me soon after I pulled off and said, "Daddy is that you I just seen talking to a hoe walking down the street?" I felt like, the audacity of the bitch trying to light weight check me. I said in a defiant tone like yeah so what, "Yeah bitch that was me, how about where are you at, so I can get my money?" She said, "I will meet you at our usual spot in ten minutes OK daddy?" Sounding stern and a little bit agitated, "Aite" I replied and hung up the cellphone. My burgundy Expedition pulled up to our usual meeting spot and J.J. was standing there waiting and talking on her cellphone. She saw me and smiled and climbed in the S.U.V. and willingly handed a brother his money. I looked at her in her face and said, "Bitch why are your eyes so watery, and your reflections so dam slow?" She answered drily, "It's from all this hoeing daddy a bitch is tired." I dug what she was saying and said, "Well bitch take a break and ride with yo pimp for a little bit, I gots to go check on Dave-baby over on the block." She got in the car and was trying to say something to me, but she fell asleep during mid-sentence. We arrived on the block, and I looked over at her while she was asleep. She was drooling from her mouth with her head in a nod. She was getting that good ole rem sleep. I didn't pay too much attention to it and jumped out the truck. Dave-baby was sitting on my old Nova, that I sold him. He was profiling while he was selling his drugs, and Spark was on the other end of the corner isolating himself from him. I noticed that Spark was looking with a "side eye." I asked, "Dave-baby, what is wrong with that nigga Spark?" He looked down for a minute like he didn't want to tell me and answered, "I don't know what the fuck is wrong with that punk ass nigga, he been actin funny toward me ever since you sold me the Nova. I think he is hatin on how much love you show me." I looked back up the block to Spark and getting ready to pull his coat tail. The detective rolls up just as I was about to call him. He stopped right in front of me and Dave-baby. He got out of his squad car and said, "You assholes know what the fuck time it is, assume the position!" We unwillingly acquiesced because we didn't want any trouble, so we did what he asked. The detective looking like one of those racist cowboys during the Indian days puts the cuffs on both of us. He flagrantly started digging for gold in our pockets and you could hear the seams of our pockets screaming. After he goes deep sea fishing in my pockets he says, "Ah, what do we have here?" as he took his hands out of my pockets holding a large sum of money. As a matter of fact, that is the money that my hoe worked hard for. Not wanting to relinquish anything to this nigga I blurted out, "I won that shooting dice at the gambling shack." The detective proudly confessed, "Welp, I just won it off of going into a dumb ass dope dealers' pocket". The detective was happy like a kid that won playing the arcade game using a 'hook' to win prizes. He checked Dave-baby's pockets with a happy face like he hit on the slot machines in Reno, but he didn't have anything on him. Because the detective came up lame, he went to Dave-baby's car and pulled out a buck knife and punctured all of his tires. I looked at Dave-baby and mouthed to him don't trip and don't say shit! As the air commence to whistle out his tires, his face appeared angry, but he kept his cool. The detective looked at me before he got back into his car and drove off with a smirk like thanks for **my** money. The funny this is, at no time did he look towards Spark up the block nope not a once. Then Spark sashayed over and said, "Man I hate that muthafucka, he always sliding through the hood fuckin with us." I rolled my eyes up in the air and said, "You mean me and Dave-baby, why don't he ever jack you?" Spark said, "I don't know maybe he never sees me or maybe he just don't like how you be shinning out here on the turf every time he comes through." He looks around and ignorantly says, "When he sees me, I be having on the same clothes lookin hella dirty and bummie he probably thinks I'm a dope fiend." As I was rubbing my wrist trying to get back circulation in them, I said, "You got a point there, if I didn't know you, I would think you was a dope fiend too." He didn't like how sarcastically I said that expression and he felt insulted, but he knew not to flex on me, because I would whoop his ass. I focused my attention to Dave-baby to call a tow truck and get his car towed to the tire shop. I would pay for it. Even though the detective took the money J.J. had just given me when we were on the track. I had a couple thousand in my wallet from when Kay-Kay and I were eating in San Francisco. While I was waiting for the tow truck to arrive to pick up Dave-baby's car, I went back in my Expedition truck to sit and wait. J.J. was still asleep but not only was she drooling from her mouth, but brown snot was coming out of her nose. I was thinking like dam and tapped her shoulder, but she would not budge. I took this opportunity while she was asleep to check her bra and run through her purse to see if she was holding out on any money. She was bone dry, not a dollar to her name. I wondered why she had so many broken balloons busted in her pursue. I thought nothing of it thinking she used it on her tricks in some kind of weird way. I opened the door and slammed it with all my force so hard that she jumped up out of her sleep. She looked around like she was scared for her life. I chuckled and said, "Bitch why are you sitting here sleep unaware of your surroundings, and clean your dam nose and wipe your fuckin mouth? Where is your class at, bitch you are starting to lose it?" She used a towelette and said, "I'm sorry daddy I was just tired from getting you your money it won't happen again." My cellphone rung, "Hello?" "What's up big brah this is Dee, can you come double me up for these five racks I got?" I responded, "Fa sho, lil-brah I see that block you getting money on in West Oakland is paying off huh?" He replied trying not to sound too cocky, "Its doing OK, it ain't like where you and Spark have it, but I can say its mines." I stated, "Just stay down making it happen you'll have workers under your wing in no time, you want to meet at the same spot?" He said, "Yeah big brah." I told him as soon as the tow truck come and I pay for Dave-baby's tires, I'll be on my way." Then we disconnected from each other. I went to restock Dee for his products, he said, "Ay man what happened to Dave-baby's car? Tow truck had to come and put new tires on it?" I told him, "Blood, it's this cop that keeps coming thru giving me and us hell on earth, plus he racist as fuck!" Dee said, "Whew I'm glad I ain't over there anymore he probably would've been jacking my ass too." Thinking about what he said I replied, "I don't know he may have left you alone, he seems not to never fuck with Spark and only me and Dave-baby incur his wrath." That's when Dee turned around with a serious look on his face and said, "Big brah watch that nigga Spark man, he is just waiting to see you fall so that he can take over the block." Before he was finishing his sentence, I was shaking my head yes and said, "I got Spark Dee don't trip." Getting agitated

I said, "I won't even be selling no more dope once I get my trucking company up and running." I said as a matter of fact. Dee shaking his head in agreement with what I had said saying, "That's what's up!" then we both "dapped" each other and he went back to his block to finish handling his business. J.J. was trying to stay awake and not fall asleep and I said, "Bitch I'm about to drop you off at home so you can get you some rest, be ready tomorrow around noon so you can get back out on the track and get me my money." She said, "O.K. daddy that's cool, that way I can be well rested for you by the afternoon when you come and get me." Once we got to her house, I had to wake her ass up again because she had fallen back asleep. When she got out the car, she dropped an unbusted balloon from under her panties. She tried to pick it up without me noticing that shit, but it was too late. I stared into her eyes and said, "Bitch what the fuck is that?" She said, "It's nothing Daddy it's just a balloon," while trying to pick it up nonchalantly. So now I hopped out my truck to see what the hell this thing is. I snatched the balloon out of her hand and pressed my fingers against it and said, "Bitch this is heroin, that's why yo stupid ass was fallen asleep with your nose running and mouth drooling you been snorting this shit! She started crying and apologizing to me, but I didn't want to hear it. She knew that no pimp wants to mess with hoes that do drugs. She knew because they would wound up being trouble in the long run. I said with disbelief, "Bitch I can't believe this shit, after all the times you told me you didn't want me to sell drugs you gone go around and start using it." She said, "Daddy a trick I was dating a few weeks ago persuaded me to use it and he told me how I would be able to hustle harder to make more money." She pleaded, "I never knew I would get addicted to it and get sick if I couldn't have it, please daddy give me one more chance. I remember when we first met, and you told me you would never forget what I have done by turning you onto the game and that you owe me. Well now, I need that favor you owe me for you to give me another chance." I felt my compassionate side starting to take over because after all, I did tell her I owed her. Abruptly I said, "Bitch I'm gone give you one more chance," with a stern look on my face. I told J.J. to take her ass in the house and I got back in my truck and took off. I was feeling some type of way, I was feeling like I needed a companion to talk to, so I called Kay-Kay. Kay-Kay answers the phone like she is not trying to wake a sleeping giant. She said in a low whisper that Boo was here, and she couldn't talk right now. I pushed the end button on my cellphone to hang it up while she was in mid speech. A strange epiphany came over me, I suddenly realized and wished that I had a woman to call my own, but I don't. As I'm driving, I'm thinking my woman is dead presidents that don't talk but look back at me. I was tripping for a minute, and I had to shake my head to shake the feeling of loneliness I felt and went back to my bachelor pad alone to take a nap.

23
CHAPTER
❖
FRESH MEAT

I told myself that I would concentrate on finding me a woman for myself that I could spoil and chill with. It's starting to get frustrating always dealing with these skanks that I seem to come across lately. I'm driving back to the house while listening to my music. As I pulled the SUV into the stall of my apartment building. Four pretty women were walking past my apartment building in the parking lot. They were looking like young models and shit. I saw this as an opportunity to do my gentleman routine, you know to see if I could catch a lady friend. I pulled into my parking spot bumping "Whatever You Want" by this bay area group. I spoke, "ladies, ladies, ladies aren't we all looking good today?" When I made that statement, I made sure I made eye contact with all of them. I continued, "You all look so good it makes a man hard to choose." The finest looking one stood in a "fast ass" stance and said, "The man better choose wisely!" I knew out of all the four pretty women, that the finest looking one seemed the most interested in me because she spoke the quickest. "Hey, my name is Big Dawg." The finest looking one said, "My name is Nina, and these are my friends. We're known as the powder puff girls." Now Nina was five one and the color of coffee with extra cream in it. Looking at her you could tell she was of an Asian Pacific American descent. Sexy black hair, body looking like a fitness model with that sexy olive complexion and perfect ass teeth. I noticed that all their eyes were glossy like J.J.'s were earlier. Nina grinned from ear to ear with the future wife line and said, "Sure do you have a number I can contact you at?" I asked, "Do you?" Looking at me like I just won the haggling she said, "How about we both just exchange numbers that way we will both have each other's hook up." We both exchanged numbers and I asked, "When is the best time to call you?" Nina said, "When is the quickest you can get to a phone?" I'm looking at her like *dam girl, you can't answer my question with a question* and said, "I will call you soon as I get settled in at my apartment." We exchanged sexy looks and went our separate ways. After I got situated at my one bedroom fully furnished bachelor's pad, I called Nina. She picked up on the first ring recognizing my number and said, "Hey handsome man" I responded with, "What's up pretty lady?" It sounded like a party in the background. I said, "Sounds like y'all doing it live over there, how can I be down?" She said, "You can be down by coming over and keeping me company." I ain't no punk so I spoke up for mines and said, "What's the apartment number?" She told me where she was located, and I went to her apartment. When she opened the door, the music was blasting, food was cooking, and Nina and her friends were half naked, and their eyes were glossy as ever! She grabbed my hand and led me to the couch. When we sat down, I saw a huge hill of powder cocaine. Now I know why their eyes were glossy and then I figured out why they call themselves the powder puff girls. I played it cool and didn't make my uncomfortableness seem obvious and started talking to Nina. I was not paying any attention to the hill of cocaine and her half naked friends. I asked ole girl, "Who's apartment is this?" Nina said, "It's all of our apartment, we are students at Cal State Hayward across the street." I couldn't believe that these pretty coke head ladies were college students, then I asked, "What is your major Nina?" While dancing to the music and the vibe with her hands in the air she said, "My major is Web Tech Engineering. I want to be able to design people's website around the world." I knew she was a smart girl, but I knew better to have a coke head as a woman. I figured I could use her to make me a trucking website for my up-and-coming company. Looking at her with tons of opportunity to take advantage of I said, "How much would you charge to make me a trucking company website for my company?" While she was spinning around like she was swiping at spider webs she said, "I won't charge you nothing at all, all you have to do is rent a web space address and I will do it from there." I put my hand on my chin and liked the idea of her being able to do it for free. I continued to conversate with her to find out more things that I could come up on. So now I'm thinking fresh meat and I must have her in my stable. She blurted out of the blue, "Do you sell?" At first, I looked at her with a hesitant look and said, "Sell what?" then she said "cocaine." I causally said, "Oh, cocaine well I don't sell it, but I buy it like that and then I cook it up and turn it into crack." She pointed her finger at me like she got the one-million-dollar question right and said, "I knew you sold something riding in that brand new Expedition Eddie Bauer with T.V.'s and rims on it with all that jewelry. I played coy and said, "How did you figure that?" So now she stopped dancing and gave me her full undivided attention and said, "Well for one thing the majority of all college students stay here, and you don't look, or dress, like the college preps. So I figured you were a dealer, when I saw you first pulled up." Wow so now I'm putting two and two together and figured out that the hunter became the hunted. She was trying to see what she could get out of me as well. I ain't mad at her so I said, "So that's it huh you only holla at me because you knew I was a coke dealer huh?" Then she grabbed me by the hand and said, "Plus you were cute too", then she said, "Do you think you can be me and my girl's supplier, so we don't have to go all the way to Oakland just to get some powder coke?" Now I'm tripping on the inside from this come up, and I was thinking *dam, how can a women look so good and have so much going for herself snort powder coke?* I did admire how Nina and her friends carried themselves with a lot of class. You sure couldn't look at them and tell, they are some powder coke users. I wondered *if she would be interested in selling her ass to make some money or to snort some extra coke*, but I would wait to spring that line on her. After weighing the pros and cons I said, "Sure I don't mind being you and your girl's supplier. I will make sure I keep some just for y'all" then she asked me if I snorted coke. Trying not to look judgmental I said, "Naw baby I don't indulge, I gots to keep my head clear to handle my business." I mean fuck I didn't lie to her. With this small tank top on with no bra and her sexy undies she walked seductively toward me and said, "Come on sexy man I'm sure a little powder coke wouldn't through you off your game, would it?" In my mind I'm already thinking that *hell I smoke too much weed, if I started snorting coke it would enhance my character and I would be crazy as hell.* I had to be quick on my feet and I hit her off with, "Rule #1 don't get high off your own supply, nah baby I'm cool." She just brushed it off like whatever and went back to enjoying her music. She picked up and used a play card to separate the hill of powder into a single line so that she could take a blow. She took a long snort and snorted the whole line in one breath. I was like dam bitch, but I found it interesting looking at her take a blow of the coke because she was so beautiful. It even made me chuckle to myself a little bit. Then when she finished, her other three friends came to the coffee table and did the same thing. They started laughing and yelling at each other and shit over the music having the party of the century just among themselves. She offered me some Chicken Chow Mein that they were cooking and since I was hungry as a dog, I accepted. To my surprise the food was very good; I was enjoying myself being around four half-naked women snorting powder. After I finished my second serving of food, I was ready for a nap which was the reason that I had left J.J. for in the first place. I told the ladies that I'll be seeing them again, as I excused myself and that I'd bring them a sample of my product tomorrow.

24
CHAPTER
❖
A REQUIEM FOR THE HOMIE

Spark and Dave-baby were still on the block after I paid for Dave-baby's tires to get fixed. Dave-baby was still getting all the customers because the dope that I give him is a better product than what Spark sales. Plus, what can I say, Dave-baby got the best customer skills. They were still on opposites sides of the corner in the neighborhood staying away from each other. Spark was getting irritated at him because of the money he was pulling in. Plus, Dave-baby had bought my Nova and was beginning to shine like me. Spark didn't want me on the block let alone another flamboyant nigga to add to the fire. So, he decided he would do something to get rid of Dave-baby once and for all. He couldn't figure out how to do it just yet. My thinking is this, *Dave-baby had a right to be on the block because he was raised out here and he worked for me so he couldn't use that excuse.* Spark would always call the detective to come and "Jack" Dave-baby and I, but they never caught us with any drugs. The only fucked up thing that was left to do, was to either take the money from us, or humiliate us in public. Some of the lookouts on the block told me this old muffed up bucket came rolling around the corner looking like a zombie car from the junk yard. It was Sparks grimy friends who pulled up saying, "Spark my main man what's the word?" Spark was shocked to see them because he thought that they may have overdosed on heroin with the money that they robbed from me. Spark looking like a smoked-out Vietnam vet says, "What's up fellas how are my favorite folks of the neighborhood?" they replied, "We could be better if you can put us up on another one of those licks you gave us a few months ago you feel me?" He had to think of something fast because if he couldn't come up with a robbery or a lick for these dudes, they would end up robbing and feasting on him! So, he was going to give them a shot at Dave-baby my protégé. He looked around like he was telling a scary story during a camp night and said, "I got another sucker for y'all to rob, and he should be worth just as much as that last nigga I turned y'all on to." His grimy patnas started to get white spit in the corners of their mouths like pit bulls getting ready to eat. The grimy patnas said, "Well who is it don't just stand there and hold it in, tell us who can we rob?" Spark said, "It's that nigga on the other end of the block that Big Dawg sold his Nova to named...Dave-baby." Feeling the shift of power Spark got more devious and said, "Is y'all down for a robbery, murder, for a few extra thousand?" These niggas were all cackling like a bunch of toothless witches and said, "How many few extra thousand?" Spark ass with a grin from ear to ear looking like the grinch said, "Five extra thousand plus whatever y'all find on that nigga." The lookouts on the block continued about what they had witness. The grimy friends came to a consensus and said, "Yeah, yeah, we can take care of that you want us to go up and smoke his ass and strip him right now?" Spark waving his hand as if somebody offered him shit on a stick said, "Naw, naw, naw that would make the block hot with homicide coming through asking a gang of questions, I got a plan we can follow through. I'm going to act like I want to squash the hostility between me and him and lure him to smoke some weed with me on a dead-end street not too far from the hood. I want y'all to be with me and sit behind him in his car. So now, when he's not paying any attention to you blow his head off then go through his pockets then we will leave him right there were he lay." His grimy patnas said, "Alright cool that sounds like a plan when are we going to handle it?" He said, "Park your car around the corner, and come toward where I am walking, and I will handle the rest." The grimy friends drove around the corner and that's when Spark walked to the other end of the corner where Dave-baby was standing. Spark walked up with a "I have a surprise for you" look and said, Dave-baby, Dave-baby how you doing homie?" He was sticking his hand out offering to shake Dave-baby's hand. Reluctantly he shook his hand and said, "What's up Spark, why are you in such a good mood all of a sudden? You was acting as if I was the last person on earth you wanted to associate yourself with." Searching for words he says, "Aw man you know how these streets can have you stressed out and shit when things aren't going your way." Acting like a politician that was caught in a lie he said, "I want to squash all the hostility between you and me by buying a tight bag of weed and letting you know I still love you like a little brother." Dave-baby appeared skeptical but accepted the offer anyway and said, "Thanks I didn't want to continue beefing with you anyway I still look up to you dog. Where do you want to go and smoke the weed at or would you rather, we just get burnt out on the block like some savages?" Feeling more and more relaxed because his plan is starting to take fruition. Spark stated, "Let's go to the dead end at the park that way we can smoke in peace and not have to worry about the police or any neighbors complaining." Like an oblivious dumb girl Dave-baby said, "Well who's car do you want to take mine's or yours?" Spark answered sarcastically, "let's take yours, because your car is "hella" clean and I got a few of my cousins from out of town who are going to smoke with us." He stated that they were from out of town, and he wanted to show them a good time. According to the block lookouts, Dave-baby body language was looking like he wasn't with it, but he decided to go on with it. Spark's grimy patnas walked up looking like hungry hyenas and stood by him not giving any eye contact to Dave-baby. He was looking just a little bit nervous and said, "Alright it's all good Spark we can hot box in my whip, y'all got the weed already?" Dave-baby asked. "Yeah, we got the weed already you know I'm like Big Dawg I keeps a good amount of weed on me." Said Spark jokingly. They all got in Dave-baby's car and headed towards the park where the dead-end street was located. Spark was sitting in the passenger seat doing small talk about how he wasn't making a lot of money on the block any more like he used to before me, and Dave-baby really started putting it down. This conversation started to make him feel uneasy and paranoid at the same time. The grimy patnas didn't say a word and just stared at Dave-baby in the rearview mirror from the backseat. They started blowing the first blunt passing it back and forth to one another and one of the grimy friends pulled out his three fifty-seven. It's possible that was the same gun he robbed and busted me in the head with. Dave-baby didn't notice that it was out in the backseat because it was concealed. While Spark was passing the blunt back to one of his grimy friends, he saw the gun out and knew what was about to happen. He said, "let me get out and take a piss" because he didn't want to get any blood on him when his grimy friend blasted the back of Dave-baby's head out. He got out and acted as if he was about to take a piss, he saw his grimy patna raise his Chrome three fifty-seven to the back of Dave-baby's head while he puffed on the blunt and pulled the trigger. BLAM!!! Was all it took, and blood and brains splattered the front window and Dave-baby's head fell to his chest. His grimy patnas got out the car and ran through his pockets and found two thousand dollars cash and calmly closed the door whipped themselves from the blood and brain particles and walked away unnoticed. Spark counted out the five thousand dollars he had promised them for the murder robbery, and they continued to walk to the block and departed their own separate ways.

25
CHAPTER
❖
LIKE A PUNCHING BAG

Kay-Kay told me later what happened after I called her unexpectantly and Boo was there. When Boo awoke, he told her that he was hungry and wanted her to cook some food for him to eat in a rude and disrespectful tone. Kay-Kay said she didn't really feel like cooking and asked if they could order something to eat in. I guess the way she said it was out of pocket and Boo got offended by her gestures. He angrily yelled, "Bitch why is it always a problem with you when I tell you to do something?" In a defiant tone she responded, "Don't nobody feel like cooking and slaving over a stove just to make you something to eat, I'm not your maid!" Boo turned around and looked at her with a matter of fact look and said, "Well bitch I ain't your personal versatile card or personal bank account either. I give you enough money to be my maid, my slave, or whatever else I want yo ass to be." Noticing that he made a valid point she said, "You don't even know how to talk to a woman to get her to do the things, you need to take classes." Seeing red he responded, "From who bitch Big Dawg?" Boo interrupted. Thinking fast on her feet she calmy said, "I was going to say from a professional Anger Management counselor, but since you say Big Dawg then yeah, you need to take classes from him then." I told her that she should've never said that. She told me that after that comment that's when things got bad. Boo lost his composure and jumped off the couch and slapped her POW! The echo sounded throughout the entire house, she swirled around and fell to the floor. Her lip started bleeding on the rug while she laid on the ground motionless and shocked from the blow just delivered to her face. As if that slap wasn't enough, he started kicking and stomping her saying, "You funky deep pussy bitch, don't you ever talk back to me when I tell yo ungrateful ass something do you hear me?" It was a rhetorical question as he kept kicking and kicking her while she laid on the ground cuddled up into a ball and covering her face with her arms to try not to get hit in the face by him stomping on her. She pleaded and cried like a slave being whooped by their master for him to stop. He didn't stop until he was tired and out of breath. He watched her laying on the floor crying and scurry herself to a corner. Then as he pointed to the kitchen he said, "Now get yo stupid ass in that muthafuckin kitchen and make me some dinner!" Of course, she acquiesced quickly and didn't say a word, got off the ground and walked into the kitchen. She opened the refrigerator and grabbed some ground meat. She thought about the time Boo told her that *he would kill her.* She was still crying sobbing and sniffling while she put the ground meat in a skillet and took out the spatula diced the meat to prepare some tacos. While she was facing the stove, she had her back to the entrance of the kitchen. She heard Boo walk up slowly behind her. She was scared to death to turn around and face him, so she kept dicing up the ground meat with the spatula. She told me that her heart was racing, thinking that he was coming back to finish the job and make good on his threat of killing her. He placed one hand on her shoulder like those mummies in scary movies and she shrieked in fear. He somberly turned her to face him and he said, "I'm sorry baby It's just that I just woke up and had a hard day's work earlier. You know how I dislike that punk ass ex-boyfriend of yours." She wanted to correct him and tell him that he brought up his name, but she digressed. Finally speaking she stated, "O.K. baby it's OK." Now that he is calm, she figured that he would have to pay for that ass whooping that she endured. Seeing that this was the perfect time to ask him for money she said, "Baby can I have some money to help my mother pay her medical bills?" The guilt made him want to make amends and he asked, with a happy tone, "How much do you need baby?" Kay-Kay crazy ass with the nine lives of cat, put extra on her Oscar performance and said, "Well, her total medical bill is two hundred thousand dollars. That's what I do with the money you always give me. So maybe ten thousand would help out a lot." He was taken back by the steepness of the price and responded, "Dam baby I said I'm trying to save my money to put a down a payment on a house. I'm really going to have to stop whipping your ass if I ever plan on doing that, because it seems as though the only way, I can forgive myself for acting like a crazy abusive boyfriend is by giving you some money." Politely nudging him she said, "Please baby I will make you feel good in the shower later on tonight if you do so." She told me that he couldn't resist her puppy dog eyes and helpless little kid voice, plus he wanted to erase the guilt he was wearing for kicking and stomping on her for no apparent reason. He contemplated it for a second and said, "Alright baby I'll go to the bank tomorrow and with-draw it from my savings account." Check mate she was thinking as she hugged him with a passionate hug, making him feel as though she forgave him. She had lured him into her trap of beating her ass again for a large sum of money. You see that was the plan all along. She manipulated him to swing on her because she knew of the pay-off and all that it entails.

Hustling is hustling no matter how you slice it…and she was a hustler. Kay-Kay planned on milking Boo until he was bone dry and then disappear, fuck him. She knew her "favorite man" meaning me would be proud of the ten thousand dollars cash she was about to hand over to me. She smiled like Michael Jackson did at the end of the Thriller video and continued to make Boo his tacos.

26
CHAPTER
❖
REALITY OF THE GAME

I finally woke up from my sleep and realized that I had slept all the way until the next day. Man, I was hella tired from all that running around and checking my traps. I got out of my California king size bed and went into the kitchen to make an oversize bowl of cereal. While eating, I heard 2 beeps letting me know that I had messages on my cellphone. I finished my cereal and then checked the messages on the cell phone. One message was from J.J. that she left last night calling to check in on her pimp. She wanted to let me know that she was sorry and that she would never snort any heroin again. The second was from Kay-Kay letting me know that she would have the money for me the next time she saw me. Look at that a playa is making money in his sleep! The third was from my business associate Spark saying something bad has happened to Dave-baby and for me to call as soon as possible. The other messages were from my late-night customers. I figured what Spark had said was the most urgent, so I called him first. "Hello, Spark what's up??" Not sounding like he was in shock or surprised he said, "Dam Big Dawg a terrible thing has happened to our little patna Dave-baby." I was feeling a since of dread and was like nigga just tell me." I impatiently said to him. "Well, what happened to him?" He said, "It's something hella fucked up that I don't want to say over the phone, come by the turf, and I'll buzz you in when you get here." I agreed then hurried and took of the clothes I had fallen asleep in and jumped in the shower, got out, and got myself ready to leave the house. I arrived there and Spark was just finishing up talking to some dudes that I had never knew he associated himself with. When these niggas rode by, they started laughing and pointing fingers at me. I paid no attention to them niggas because I was too worried about what had happened to homie Dave-baby. I walked up to him and said, "What Spark I got here as quick as I could, now what was you saying about Dave-baby?" This nigga is a terrible actor, and he tried to look depressed and sad as he said, "Man somebody killed our little patna Dave-baby" I was shocked with disbelief because I had just seen this man…alive! I guess I was in denial and refused to believe it, so I said, "Ay man don't fuck with me like that blood, death is nothing to play around with." Spark said, "I'm serious." Spark describes the killing and says, "looked like somebody shot him in the back of the head while he was sitting in his car." I had a look on my face like I was incoherent of the news that he was telling me. He continued to say, "And the cold thing about it is, he is still sitting in the Nova with his head blown off down at the dead end at the park." I snapped out of my incoherent trance and said, "Take me to him." We jumped in my S.U.V. and headed to where his body was at. We arrived there and Dave-baby looked like he was asleep with his head tucked into his chest. The coroner's got him out of the car and examined the body at the crime scene. I started to break down and Spark showed no remorse of any kind. I'm hella angry now and I said, "Dam, Spark who the fuck would what to do something like this to Dave-baby?" Spark with his nonchalant attitude said, "Man you never know, maybe it was some dope fiends that tried to rob him." My inner thoughts are giving me a bunch of scenarios and I say, "Dope fiends who tried to rob him huh?" Mistakenly I let it spew out of my mouth. "Whoever it was, Dave-baby must've trusted them enough to let them sit in the car seat behind him; it's obvious that it had to be two or more people. Dave-baby ain't finna go to the park and chill with no dope fiends." Spark zipped his lips before his mouth wrote a check his ass couldn't cash. "**Fuck!**" I said out loud to relieve some frustration that was built up inside me. "We gots to call the ambulance and get him up off of these streets like this," I said. Spark response is now we are going to have to answer hella questions from 5-0 now. At once I'm fucking irritated about the situation and said, "So what, we'll answer any question they want to know, and how did you know where the body was?" I demanded. Looking stupid and trying not to incriminate himself he answered, "Some dope fiends came and told me earlier this morning." I said, "Your fucking answer to everything is always some dope fiends told you some shit, nigga did they tell you who killed him?" Spark looking nervous said, "Naw man calm down they didn't tell me who killed him, but I know I'm not gone be here to answer no questions that homicide gone be here to ask us." While headed to a phone booth a few blocks down I knew the block was going to be on fire, since the death of Dave-baby, and I didn't want to get caught up. I dropped Spark off at his cousin house and decided not to hang out on the block for a while to play it safe.

27

CHAPTER

❖

CHANGE OF DIRECTION

I thought about the time my oldest brother told me about Las Vegas. The only thing is who would I be able to take to Vegas to get money with me? J.J. wasn't classy enough and now that I discovered she was snorting heroin, she definitely wasn't Vegas material. I'm going to find somebody to go with me and get this Vegas money. My cellphone started ringing and it was J.J. I hesitantly picked it up and said, "Bitch what's up?" Trying to fast talk me like a salesman she says, "Daddy I'm kicking this heroin jones I got, my stomach is killing me plus I got the shits. Do you think you can bring me some Pepto-Bismol to help me kick it faster so I can get out on the track today?" I cut her off on the phone and said, "Bitch that's what your stupid ass gets for snorting that bull-shit. I'll go by the store and get it when I'm finished handling my business." With a nervous laughter she said, "Okay daddy thank you I'll be here waiting on you so I can make this up to you by hoeing my heart out!" While she was saying all of that shit I was looking like yeah right. I said, "Alright bitch" and hung up the phone. I called Kay-Kay to see what was up with the ten thousand dollars she said she had for me. "Hey baby how are you doing this morning?" with my Barry White deep voice. "I'm doing O.K. Baby did you get my message?" she said. Yeah, I got it this morning when I woke up, how the hell did you come up with ten thousand dollars?" She said, "Baby if you only knew what I go through to fuck with this trick ass nigga Boo. I don't want to upset you so the less you know, the better off you will be." I said, "Dam baby, that bad huh, well is it cool if I come thru to come holla at you for a little while, plus I need to check my stash and make sure everything is OK." She said, "It's cool baby, his ass is gone to work, he went to his account this morning to give me the money before he left." I said, "I'm on my way, I could use a little cheering up if you know what I'm talking about, my patna Dave-baby was found dead in his car today and I'm doing a little grieving." She replied slyly, I'm about to start exercising my tongue and jawbones now baby so I can suck you dry." I arrived at her house and went straight for my stash. Sorry but no time for pleasantries until I see, count, and feel my dough. I gathered all my shit like I usually do and counted all of my money and weighed all of my dope. I spread it all on the table to get an accurate count. Once I finished, I said, "It's all there." Then Kay-Kay immediately got the ten thousand dollars, she gave it to me and got down on her knees. I hurried up and pulled my dick out and held it like a porn star as she commenced to suck my manhood. She started off licking the tip with her tongue and kissed the shaft with her lips. She held my balls in her hand, then buried her face in them. She sucked and sucked while I grunted and talked shit to her. She handled her business like a true veteran. After thirty minutes of slurping licking and sucking I released my load in her mouth. She swallowed it all as usual not letting a drop fall to the ground, then kissed my balls, shaft and tip for another 5 minutes. She was showing me how she loves my jewels. When she was done pleasing me, she got up off of her knees and said, "Baby you want me to cook you some breakfast?" I said, "Naw pretty lady, I gots to go handle some business with this bitch J.J. so she can get me my money." "Oh" she said, "How is the pimpin holding up for you?" she asked. "It's cool baby it's a lot harder than I thought and I'm only at the beginning stage of it. I already caught the bitch treating her nose with some heroin and don't know what to expect next from the bitch." She smiled and said, "Daddy you ain't gone get rich overnight pimpin, maybe you should start lookin for another hoe to replace her or start putting other hoes on your team." I was thinking that ole girl has a point and I said, "You sure no what I should do, why don't you start turning some of these tricks for me so that we can get to the top. I would feel a lot more comfortable in the game with you by my side." Then she got a little bit uncomfortable and answered, "I would get down with you, but I'm scared to shit of meeting some random man. I know nothing about him and letting him have his way with me for a few hundred dollars, that nigga could be a psycho killer! I'm not feeling that. She continued, at least with these boyfriend tricks, I'm the one running shit. I just let them think they are running shit and they have me in control, but I'm really plotting on the whole bank account or whatever I feel is valuable to me." I reassured her by rubbing her face and said, "It's cool baby I can respect it, every woman has their own way of getting money its nothing I can say about that just as long as I'm eating, my mouth is shut." She smiled at me with relief, and I slapped her on her ass and told her to put the stash up for me. I grabbed some powder coke for Nina and the powder puff girls. I also picked up some hard crack for my late-night clientele. I knew for sure that I would be serving because the hood was going to be hot due to Dave-baby's death.

28
CHAPTER
❖
TIME TO PAY THE PIPER

Kay-Kay said that she would put it up after she walked me to the SUV. We indulged in a passionate kiss in front of my Expedition, right when Boo was coming back. I have to admit I was slipping. I should've never done PDA (public, display, of Affection) especially in front of her dam house. I should've just told her no need to walk me to the truck and then bounced! Boo came for his work jacket that he forgot at her house. Little did I know, Boo sat in his truck probably with steam coming thru his ears and heat coming from the top of his head. He had never seen my Expedition truck before and thought it may have been some other man kissing his woman. I turned around to get into my truck, and he realized it was me. He started banging his hands on the steering wheel with his fists, yelling inside the truck. I paused like well what you wanna do? He just sat there heated, so I bounced and got back into traffic. Unbeknownst to Kay-Kay waving good-bye to her "favorite man" and blowing kisses at the same time. She did not know the level of anger, rage, and violence that she was about to occur. Sashaying up the stairs, dancing and singing and smiling in love, but little did she know that her day was about to get interrupted. I called her on the cellphone, but it was in the house, and she didn't get a chance to answer my call. Later on, she told me how everything went down after I left. She said, Boo got out his truck and ran right behind her like a raging gorilla and said, "Bitch I thought you wasn't fuckin wit that punk ass nigga!" *I could imagine her running just like that scene from boys in the hood when Ricky tried to turn and run away before he got shot.* She was frightened, startled, and surprised and turned around to see Boo stampeding towards her with fire in his eyes. She tried to run up the stairs to get to the doorway to close the door to try and lock him out until he cooled down. She was running and falling up the stairs for her life, she was thinking, if she could just make it inside and regroup to do her thing about calming him down, she would be ok. But because she knew he was going to kill her or beat her to a comatose state. She feared that she was finished. When she was running to the door, he was gaining on her and was able to thrust his foot in the doorway to make the door jam. With the help of his adrenaline, he pushed the door back and sprung himself inside the house breathing like a gorilla. With no words he balled his fist up… and hit her square in her mouth like she was man. She dropped to the ground in a heap screaming, begging, and pleading with him to let her explain. She was trying to reach for the phone to call the police and he snatched the phone out of the socket. Boo looked on the table with amazement and saw the money and dope sprawled out all over the table. He put two and two together and started stomping and kicking her. He kicked her in her ribs, her back, her but, her stomach, her face, her shoulder, and stomped on her hands all the while asking that rhetorical question, "Bitch I thought you wasn't fucking with him huh…huh?" Fighting for her survival she was spitting out blood from the hit he delivered to her mouth with clumps of hard particles coming out and she realized it was her teeth. She was yelling for him to stop and tried to scare him by saying she was going to call the police. It did no good and fell on deaf ears. Some moments he would stop only to take a break, and when he got his second and third wind, commenced to beat, kick, and stomp her until she began to look unrecognizable. He continued to kick and stomp her until she was unconscious. When she came to, she cried, and her face was swollen and battered, and she could barely move. Boo was over at the table were the dope and money were sprawled out at. He couldn't believe that I had so much money and drugs at Kay-Kays's house. He went to the kitchen drawer and pulled out a butcher knife. He took the knife and went to her and snatched her up by her hair. She said she was screaming, No, No please!? He put the knife to her neck and said, "Bitch I should kill yo ass right here were you lay." She started pleading saying she was sorry as he held the knife to her throat. Boo thought of something much worse that he could do to her…to me. With his twisted smile he thought of a perfect way to get back at me. He devised a plan to hit me where it hurts by kidnaping Kay-Kay and taking all the drugs and money. He wanted to make it seem like she picked up and left with all of my shit. He made her get up and pack an overnight bag and grabbed all of my money and dope. He forced her to put it in a garbage bag. Hoping that she would try and make a move he held the knife to her back and made her walk out the doorway and into his truck. He would come back to move out her furniture and secured the house. They would leave the scene enroute to who knows where.

29
CHAPTER
❖
ENTER PIMP-OLOGY

I went to the drug store and purchased J.J. some Pepto-Bismol so that she could kick her morning heroin jones. I hoped back into my truck and went to her house and called when I was out front. She came outside to get the medicine and asked if I wanted to come in. I smoothly declined, and said, "I would rather wait in the car and hurry up and come back out." So, she hurried up, showered, got dressed, and swallowed half of the Pepto-Bismol and came back outside in twenty minutes. She looked a lot better than she did yesterday dozing off and shit looking half dead. When she got inside the car she said, "Thank you daddy for getting me the Pepto-Bismol and still believing in me" with schoolgirl innocence. I kept looking at the road and said, "J.J. even though we are in the game together I'm still your friend, I will help you no matter what state of mind you're in, just as long as you're willing to help yourself." She was happy that we were cool again and hugged her pimp as her eyes got filled with tears. But before the tears could fall completely, I said, "O.K. bitch enough of this square business shit. Let's get back to this pimpin and hoeing." She smiled and laughed slightly because she knew that was my way of letting her know that I forgave her. She said, "Alright daddy where we off to?" I said in a stern tone, "Bitch we been going to High Street long enough, it's time for us to step our game up just a little. I figure we can go to Frisco and warm the track up out that way and see what type of money you can come up with. I know it's kind of early, but tricks still want to have fun during their lunch hours and after work." With a rejuvenated spirt she said, "Well let's roll out daddy I'm always down for new challenges," and we headed to Frisco. Traffic was a bitch, but we finally made it through all the traffic on the San Francisco bridge and got to the spot. The Frisco track was a lot worse than the track in Oakland. The cars and limos that road up and down the track told me that it may be a little more beneficial. I gave J.J. her pep talk, I mentioned where our meeting spot would be, then told her to get out and get it! She was fired up and jumped out the SUV in front of five other hoes. She started waving and blowing kisses to the cars and limos that were driving up and down the street. I smashed off and parked my SUV truck on a narrow alley and walked back to the track where all the action was. As I was walking on the track, I observed everything happening because I knew hoe tracks are not alike. There were bums on the street, weed dealers, coke dealers, and heroin dealers making their daily quota. I noticed some hoes were well dressed up in high heels and skirts. These hoes were taking the game way more serious than the hoes on the Oakland track. I wished J.J. could stay strong and not get overwhelmed by the heroin dealers who were so easily accessible to her. I thought to myself *I better watch her* and strolled my way into a small, secluded pool hall to shoot some 8 ball. As I entered the pool hall everyone who was talking stopped to look at me. Once they realized I wasn't a cop, they returned to their conversations. I had to break a bill for the pool table and racked up the balls. I'm just chilling playing a game of pool all to myself and I observed the crowd. I peeped game that there were other pimps, and hustlers who were talking business. After about thirty minutes of me being at the pool hall the doors opened and the people in the crowd got quiet again and looked at who was coming through the door. We noticed it wasn't 5-0 and everybody went back to their business. This dude that walked in was greeting everybody shaking hands and talking slicker then oil. He had a suit on and some gators with a brim hat on his head. I just figured with his character that dude got to be a pimp, because he fit the profile of one. He walked over to the table where I was shooting pool and said, "Say young pimpin, is that yo hoe out there waving and blowing kisses at the cars driving by?" I was thinking aww shit here we go and responded, "I don't know who you talking about pimp." I ain't met none of these dudes formally and I was not wanting to let another pimp that I haven't seen before knowing my business. The other pimp said, "Well, my five bitches that's out hoeing right now said the bitch jumped out of your burgundy Expedition." I stopped shooting pool and held the stick against my body just in case I had to swing on this nigga with it and said, "Why, what's it to you pimpin if she is my bitch or not?" So now the pimp facial expression changed to being irritated and said, "Check this out bruh, I'm not trying to tell you the bitch is out of pocket or no shit like that, but with all that waving and blowing kisses and shit, the bitch is going to burn the track up or worse, catch herself a hoe case." I responded, "Pimpin let me tell you something main, don't nobody come and tell me how to have my bitch get my money, I'm the teacher, instructor, and the professor when it comes to my bitch getting my money ya dig?" The pimp looked around and got tickled and said, "listen young pimpin, I've been on this track getting money since a grasshopper, I know you are new out here and I was just trying to give you a little advice my gee." I had felt hostile and said "Man yo advice ain't needed, so you can take yo ass somewhere else with that shit and let me tend to my pool game!" The pimp took a step back and readjusted his hat and said, "Hey you right young pimpin, my bad I thought you was one of those up-and-coming young pimps that knew how to listen to somebody that's been in the game for a while." The pimp then turned around laughing and walked out the door. I started thinking *maybe I need to peep game because he didn't ask me for anything. He was just trying to teach me "pimp-ology" but I was being a hot head.* I called J.J. on her cellphone and got no answer. So, I thought she may have been busy taking care of a trick to get his money. I called my brother Big Bruh to get some advice on whether or not I should have listened to the other pimp about J.J. out there hoeing, and blowing, kisses and waving. As always in his loud and boisterous voice, "What's up lil brah, what can I do for you?" I said, "I'm out here on the track in San Francisco right, and I was wondering if my bitch should be out here hoeing, blowing tricks kisses, and waving at them when they drive by?" Gasping like that was one of the cardinal rules to break Big Bruh said, "Hell naw little brah that bitch can easily get her ass wrapped up by the police or burn herself up! He continued, "Every track is different remember me telling you that?" He further stated, "On a track like Frisco the bitch can wear hoe gear, but she can't be so obvious about what she's doing. You need to call the bitch and tell her to cool it with that Oakland High St. hoeing, and just chill and let the tricks approach her." Thinking I better go get her right now I said, "Thanks Big Bruh Ima hit you back later!" I should've made haste to go and get her but, I decided to stay and finish my pool game for another twenty minutes. I don't see her on the track, so I attempted to call her again. A man's voice answered on the line saying, "Yeah who's this?" I felt disrespected that a trick would answer her phone, so I instantly went off cussing at the man and asked where's J.J.? Dude on the other line seemed less impressed and said, "Who is this?" Now I'm fired up and I say, Nigga this is her muthafuckin pimp!" That is my investment right there, and I was thinking that she was in some trouble getting sweated by another pimp. The dude replied with a smirk in his voice, "Ohhhh, so J.J. is her real name, well guess what asshole you just confirmed that your lady is out here prostituting." Then he spoke up with a grand introduction and bass all in his voice and shit and said, "This is Officer Bob Parr for the San Francisco City Vice Squad, your hoe is on her way to jail. With a dumb ass invitation he asked, "Would you like to join her for a pimping and pondering case?" I was mad as fuck and hung up the phone. Now I was spooked thinking that the police knew where I was. I didn't know if they were going to bust up in the pool hall and take me to jail on pimping and pondering charges. The doors of the pool hall swung open making a buzzing sound when somebody comes through the door. Everybody looked up especially me, then everyone resumed what they were doing. Now I know why people looked at me when I first came up in here. They all thought that they were going to take that ride to the station. I left the pool stick on the pool table and headed out the door. I was walking to the car feeling some type of way thinking about how Dave-baby got killed, and then I felt it was my fault that J.J. got arrested. I couldn't believe that I blew her cover by giving the police her real fucking name. Just as I was walking the pimp that I had a few words with inside the pool hall, was standing by his big body 500 SL Mercedes Benz. He was looking at me with the look like I -told- you- so and said, "Say young pimpin keep your head up it's all a part of the game. You gone send plenty bitches to jail before you get the game right." While finishing up eating crow I said, "Man O.G. I shouldn't have been so stubborn and took your advice." He appeared to accept my apology and said, "Young pimpin you sort off did the right thing, you don't know me from the man in the mirror." My attention quickly turned to how am I going to get my bitch out of jail. The pimp decided to introduce himself to me and said, "I'm Stay Paid young pimpin" with his hand extended out for a handshake. I didn't have no pimp name, so I said with pride, "They call me Big Dawg." I reached out and shook his hand firmly. Stay Paid is a five-foot nine pimp legend, always wearing shades, with a perfect lined goatee, and his clothes are colorful and always clean as fuck! Little did I know that I was in the presence of royalty in the pimp game. We shook hands and Stay Paid said, "The first thing you need to do is get in touch with a bail bondsman to get your bitch back, if you don't know of one, I got somebody for you." I'm thinking like *dam ain't this some shit?* I curiously asked, "How much is the bond going to be?" Stay paid was admiring himself and said, "Well young playa, it all depends on if this is your bitches first hoe case or if she has any priors of any kind." As he was adjusting his Gucci glasses he said, "Or if you have some collateral that you own." Dam, I don't own shit like that yet. Finally, he gave me the number to the bail bondsman. I said, "Thanks Stay Paid, how can I pay you back for this favor you just done for me, by helping me get my bitch back?" The pimp answered, "By just staying down with the game young pimpin, if there is anything I can do for you don't be too stubborn to ask." That was some good news for me, and I gave the pimp some dap and sprinted to my SUV.

30

CHAPTER

❖

A FAUX STALLION

Driving from Frisco to Oakland my cell started ringing. I answered it not recognizing the number hoping it was Dee calling me for some more double-up action. Eagerly I picked up my phone and said, "Hello?" A female's voice I didn't recognize said, "Hey handsome tennis shoe pimp, this is Sasha do you remember me?" Riding in my SUV with an awe expression on my face, but I didn't want to let her know I was so surprised. I slyly said, "Yeah bitch I remember you, you that bitch that I met at the doughnut shop in the town on High Street that gave me that hundred dollars for conversation. She started to giggle like the jig is up and said, "Yep that's me, are you still accepting new applications for new hoes?" Her voice exalted with happiness because I remembered who she was. She was that sexy ass stallion bitch from the coffee shop. "Of course, I'm accepting bitch as long as the choosing fee is a sufficient amount of funds" I said. Not wanting to miss this moment on being on my team she said, "I have twenty-five hundred on me right now, plus I'm out here on High Street still hoeing. You can come get it now if you aren't too busy" she said. I had to hit the switch on her ass and said, "Bitch who said that was enough money for me as a choosing fee?" She was taking back by this I could tell, and she said, "Oh I'm sorry." Truth be told she was admiring how I was conducting myself like a seasoned pimp. Gathering her senses she said, "Is twenty-five hundred enough Daddy?" I sat back on the phone in silence for a minute because, that was way more than enough money for her choosing fee. I acted as if it wasn't, and I grumbled under my breath. I said, "Yeah bitch that's cool, but I usually get at least three gees since you out there hoeing already. You can pay back the five hundred that you are missing with interest. I'll come and get the money now then pick you back up at a designated time and place to get the rest. Meet me at the doughnut shop were we first met, and I'll be there in about fifteen or twenty minutes. Before I hung up the phone with her, I demanded, "And don't ever call me a tennis shoe pimp again, bitch you're here with me!" Not wanting any smoke with me she acquiesced and said, "OK daddy," and hung up the phone. I arrived at the doughnut shop on High Street to get my money from Sasha twenty minutes after I had talked to her. I walked inside the coffee shop, and was a little bit shocked to find that she was sitting at the table like instructed waiting for me to walk in. When she saw me, she tried to hand me the money all out in the open. I got pissed and said, "Bitch what the fuck is wrong with you, don't give me any money out in the open like that, this shit ain't legal!" I was hella mad at her stupid ass for doing some goofy shit like that and said, "These muthafucka people know you're a hoe and that I'm pimpin with you. What the fuck pimp did you have before that let you do some dumb shit like that in public on a hoe stroll?" Then She said, "Oops sorry daddy I wasn't thinking, I was just happy you came thru and to see you." I turned up my nose and said, "Well bitch I don't need you to think I need you to be a hoe and pay me to think for you now follow me around the corner to my Expedition and we can handle our business in there." She leaped up seeing that I was serious about my pimpin and walked behind as we went to the car. We got into the car, and she said, "I got the rest of the chosen fee daddy, the whole three gees." I got to be cautious and watch my back, so I asked her ass, "Bitch how the fuck did you get an extra five hundred in twenty minutes? Do you think I'm stupid bitch? Strip of all your fuckin clothes right now!" She hesitantly began to strip down and an extra one thousand dollars slipped out of her panties. Now I'm looking at this bitch like we already starting off on the wrong foot. I said, "Bitch what the fuck you holding out for?" I didn't even wait for a response and slapped her across her face. She was stunned and said, "I'm sorry Daddy that was the money for my rent. I live in a one bedroom. I turn tricks out of an apartment on MacArthur she said embarrassedly." She must really got the game messed up. I told her, "Bitch you don't pay your rent I do, don't ever hold out on me like that do you hear me?" With her eyes filled with tears and regretting that she chose me, she whispered Okay. I guess I was way too sharp for her than her other pimp before. I looked at her in disgust and said, "Bitch, what's your other pimps cell number so that I can call him and serve him your walking papers." She happily gave me the number and I called homeboy. "Who dis?" Sasha ex pimp said. "This is Big Dawg pimpin, I was giving you the respect to give you a courtesy call to let you know that Sasha is no longer your bitch. She chose me pimpin and I'm keeping it real." Dude on the other line didn't know what to say and responded, "What that bitch don't want to fuck with me no moe?" I had to reassure him like naw bruh this ain't no joke and said, "Naw pimpin she done chose me with a beneficial choosing fee of four thousand plus she gone get way more for me." I didn't want to come off as a hostile takeover, but I had to let him know how this was going down and said, "I need the bitch's clothes that you have so she can continue smashing to get my ration." That didn't sit well with her ex-pimp, and he said, "Fuck that! I ain't given you or that bitch her clothes she just gave you four thousand dollars, and the bitch would take dam near a month just to give me that. So, you buy that bitch some clothes with that money nigga." I laughed at homeboy and said, "Well fuck it then pimpin, since you want to be a poor sport about the bitch jumping ship and choosing me, then you wear the hoes clothes." All pleasantries went out of the window, and he angrily said, "Nigga I'm gone kill you and that bitch, don't let me catch you slipping out here." I responded with a calm demeanor and said, "This is gentleman's game pimpin, if you feel you want to kill somebody over these no good funky sticking ass hoes, then you need to find yourself another line of business." I disconnected the line and was hoping that I don't get a target on my back for this one. I didn't know where my aggressive attitude toward the game came from suddenly. I presumed that this is what happens when you start really getting your feet wet with the pimpin, and it just comes naturally. It may have come over me because I found Dave-baby dead, or because J.J. had gone to jail, or the thrill of knocking a new hoe and serving her pimp his walking papers. Well, whatever caused me to have this aggressiveness it was no turning back now fuck it. My phone rung and I answered, "What's up big timer how can I be down?" Dee was fired up and said, "Big brah the spot is rolling hella hard, I need you to bring me some double-up action as soon as you can." So, I'm juiced for my nigga and said, "Foe show how much do you need some action for?" Without hesitation he said, "four thousand." I said, "I'll see you in about fifteen or twenty minutes" and hung up the phone. Sasha and I arrived at the spot where I usually meet Dee for our exchanges. Sasha was even more fascinated by seeing how much money I had made in one sell. She liked when other pimps had other hustles instead of relying on her to bring in the money. She liked that fact because, it would take a lot of pressure off her. She wouldn't make any mistakes while she was out on the track hoeing. Sizing me up she said sheepishly, "Daddy what does your other bitch look like?" I ran the description of J.J. all the way down to the Jay-lo ass and said, "Bitch what you want to know for?" She looked at me with a don't judge me look and said, "Because daddy I like to eat pussy and feel the compassion of another woman when I'm on somebody's team." Ecstatically I said, "Bitch is that right, I don't think the bitch I have now gets down like that, but we will find you a bitch to bring home real soon." She asked, "Are we going back to the track daddy?" I contemplated it for a sec and then responded, "Naw, your ex-daddy might be lurking in the cut to catch me or you slipping. I tell you what, we just gone lay low for a few days until he knocks him a new bitch and finds himself some other business." Impatiently she said, "Well where are we going to go today daddy?" I said, "San Francisco." We drove on to the freeway to go back over the bay bridge to get this money. I parked my truck and gave her the run down. I told her to call me in 3 hours to check in so that

I could take the money she had on her. She got out on the track about to start blowing kisses and waving. I stopped her real quick and told her not to hoe like she does in Oakland or else she will get all of us busted. I should've told her the story about J.J. going to jail but decided against it. I didn't want to come across as being new to the track and having no proper guidance for her. I walked on over to the pool hall to shoot some pool and to try and ease my mind a little bit. The cell started ringing again and I looked at the caller I.D. I perked up because I realized that it was the fine ass college chick that snorts hills of powder. I confidently answered and said, "Hey pretty lady." You could hear her smile over the phone, and she responded, "Hi handsome I guess you already knew who this was by answering the phone with such a sweet compliment as that." Getting myself ready for the good news I responded, "Of course I do sweetheart, I know your number by heart already, and I just met you yesterday." While aw gollying Nina said, "I feel so special." Me being the player that I am stated, "As of right now you are the most specialist woman on my list." I was lying like a muthafucka, then I heard a loud crash, boom, boom, crash then her phone dropped, and I heard screaming. I was thinking like oh shit what just happened. I yelled, 'Nina, Nina, Nina but I got no response. I could hear her voice and stayed on the line to see what happened. When she finally came back to the phone she was crying and saying she wrecked her car! Concerned of course I asked, "Are you alright? with a concerned voice then She answered, "No I'm not alright." She was crying and getting ready to go into the hysterical stage and said, "I don't have any physical injuries wrong with me, but my car is totally wrecked in the front, and I don't have insurance." Where the hell is the other car that wrecked into it, maybe they have insurance?" As she was crying, she said, "Nope, they ran into my car then took off before I could get the license plate, now I have to call the police." Like a scene from a bad movie, reality is hitting hard for her, and she asks, "How I'm I going to pay to get my car fixed?" I figured that this was a perfect time to get her to come to Las Vegas with me to get some money and said, "Calm down baby everything's going to be alright, I think I have a way for you to get your car fixed but it all depends on how far you are willing to go and what you are willing to do." While she is wiping her nose she mutters, "I'll do anything, I just got this car and I still owe a couple thousand dollars on it." Looking like I'm getting ready to say UNO in a card game I said, "I will tell you about it when I come and pick you up a little later. I still have a sample of my product that I was going to give you. Maybe that will help cheer you up? I told her that, "I'll call a tow truck and have the car towed to my apartment building and wait for you there." After reassuring her I continued to shoot ball at the pool hall. After an hour and thirty minutes had passed, I left the pool hall and headed to a small mom and pops crab shack. After I finished eating it would be time for me to go meet up with her to take the money she made and add it to the rest of the clump of money I had in my pocket. As I sat cracking crab and eating a salad, the thoughts of my big-time trucking company filled my imagination. *I daydreamed of a purple Volvo big rig; the name of my trucking company Class A trucking imbedded on the sides of the trailer.* I was thinking that man, *I would transport anything from hazardous material, to produce, anywhere cross country as long as the pay was right.* I figured I could have more than one truck and could have a few employees under me. I have big dreams when it came to reaching my goal of owning my own trucking company. Hell, I even figured I could move to Las Vegas because the instructor at the trucking school told me it's a lot of money for truckers in Las Vegas because they're always building and destroying casinos on a regularly basis. While I was still in "la la land" about my dream, it was interrupted with a ring from this dam cellphone. At first, I didn't want to answer it because it was a restricted number, but I decided to go ahead because it could be some money opportunity, or it could be important. A voice that sounded familiar to me said, "Hello? Young pimpin, young pimpin, young pimpin!" The voice belonged to my new pimp patna that came over the phone. Recognizing who it was I respond with, "What's up pimpin, you calling me to let me know my bitch got bonded out from your bail bondsman man?" The mood of the call changed, and he said, "Naw pimpin he ain't called and told me yet you might want to call down there and see if he's gotten her yet. Hopefully he not just letting the bitch sit around drinking coffee in his office and chilling inside the holding tank." I appreciated the info and said, "I'll do that, I'll do that but check this out how did you get my number pimpin?" The pimp took a deep breath and said, "Pimpin, the bitch man, the bitch Sasha man. She said she don't want to be pimpin for you no more man. The bitch is sitting here right now, and she done gave me the money she made since she was out here." On the inside I was thinking *that's poet justice* and said, "Dam, I guess this is a courtesy call letting me know you knocked my hoe," and I started laughing like I was at a comedy show. The pimp wasn't shocked or surprised that I was laughing because he knew a real young pimp when he saw one and started laughing with me. Finally, after laughing like a maniac, I calmed down and asked, "Did you knock my other bitch keep it 100?" he said "Now man I did try though, when I first saw the bitch blowing kisses and waving at the tricks driven by. My hoes had told me where the bitch was, but she wasn't trying to hear a word I was saying. She got away from the pimpin like it was a disease." Feeling like I was dunked in one of those dunk tanks games at the fair I said, "It's all good pimp, fuck that hoe I just knocked the hoe about 5 hours ago and had to call her ex-pimp with a courtesy call you feel me?" Now you serve me with one about this trick ass hoe." In agreement the pimp nodding his head said, "Oh like that young pimpin? I already see what kind of hoe this bitch is. She's one of them choose Suzie bitches that gets nowhere in the game because she keeps jumping ships. I wouldn't be surprised if the bitch is just mad at her ex-pimp, and he caught her playing games. I'm gone make this bitch hoe for forty-five hours straight because I no she is a quick cop and blow." With much respect I said, "Alright pimp, O.G. pimpin, let me catch this bail bondsman to see what's up with my bottom bitch, you can lock my phone number in your phone if you want to." It looks like I'm gone be seeing you around for a while and you know **pimpin gots** to stick together." His octaves went back up and he said, "Gotcha young pimpin and you do the same!" Right before I hung up on that ass though I said, "And oh yeah pimpin I owe you one!" He laughed for a little bit and said, "That's right young pimpin you owe me one." I finished up my crab, salad, and drunk a bottle of Moet then left the Crab Shack. I reached out to the bail bondsman about J.J., and he said she was safe with him and that he needed to meet me at his office. He needed to get the fee for the bail and the collateral for the bond together. I told him that I was on my way and that I would see him in fifteen or twenty minutes. Arriving at the bail bondsman office, I was happy to see J.J. and she was just as happy to see me. The bail bondsman is a capital 'D' shaped white dude that only cares about the "dollar dollar bill y'all." He looked like he has been a sleaze for years. He wore khaki pants that looked like he bought them from Walmart, a short-sleeved shirt that was dingy, and he had on some suspenders to keep his pants over his belly. Anyway, he coughed at me and said fifteen hundred dollars for the bail and the pink slip from my Expedition for the bond. I knew J.J. was well worth the money and wouldn't miss her court dates. The bail bondsman gave me his private cell number and told me that he could bail anybody out of jail no matter what city or state they were in. I took the card and told her let's go and gave my new bondsman a handshake and told him it was nice to meet you and do business with you. So now we are out and feeling hella good. I thought to myself, "dam lose a hoe gain a hoe looks like another hoe T.K.O." J.J. thanked her pimp for being there once again. We got inside the car she said, "Daddy look" and I looked. She proceeded to bring some moist wet money out of her pussy. "Shit, I said, that money stank like a pound of shrimp." Looking proudly like she just caught a big ole catfish she said, "It's a dirty game daddy and dirty money." That money smelled like fresh fish at one of those fish stands. I asked, "How much is that?" She said "Its two thousand dollars daddy and I wasn't even out there longer than an hour! The Frisco track crank hella hard, I don't give a fuck if I got busted, I'm ready to go back out there and hoe some moe." Man hearing some shit like that made my love for J.J. grow even more knowing she didn't get out of pocket when that pimp tried to knock her. I was chilling and driving and thinking about the heart she had to get back out there and still hoe after she got busted. I let her know, "It's cool baby, I mean bitch we'll go back out there in a few days. Let's let the heat cool off a bit in the meantime I'm going to treat you to some crab and noodles at Crustaceans, even though I already ate." Her face lit up and she said, "Thank you daddy!" Then she told me she loved me. I didn't tell her back, but she already knew how a brutha felt about her and I didn't have too. She just looked at me like a sweet 16 crush and rode in the car with blissfulness and contentment.

31
CHAPTER
❖
GUESS WHO'S COMING TO VEGAS?

I turn my attention to Nina. I'm thinking of a master plan to get her on board with the pimping in Vegas. I wanted to see what the best possible approach to get Nina to prostitute her body out in Las Vegas. I called to let her know I was on the way and that I would be there in fifteen to twenty minutes. I arrived at her apartment and knocked on the door. It took a while like 10 Mississippi's to answer the door then, she asked, "Who is it?" in a distressed voice. I was hoping that she wasn't physically damaged because she might just be on my team. I said, "Dam baby. I almost didn't recognize you." She wasn't hurt or anything like that, but you could tell that she had been going through it. Her body language was like "blah" and rightfully so. She said, "Come on in Big Dawg, I'm so depressed and frustrated I don't know what to do." Trying to lighten the mood I said, "Oh baby it's going to be Okay, I'm here to console you back to good spirits." With a devilish grin. Not processing what I just said, she led me to the couch in the living room. I saw that the whole house was atrocious! It was cups with half liquor in them, clothes thrown all over the place, and plates of molded food that had been sitting on coffee tables. I had to shake off the dirty house and get down to business and said, "Is this a good time for you to test the product I have?" She looked up at me and said, "Hell yeah it is!" She was starting to perk up a little bit and explained, "My friends are in class right now, so I can snort without sharing." She said with a smile. I proceeded to pull out a small amount of powder cocaine out of my pocket and handed it to her. With glee she took off like a flash and went to the kitchen and grabbed a small silver spoon out of the drawer. She put some of the cocaine on the spoon and took a deep full-blown snort. Then she said, "Whew, this cocaine just exploded in my brain like dynamite!" I stand by my product, so I said, "Is that a good thing or a bad thing?" While wiping her nose and sucking on that same finger as if it was icing from a cake. Delightfully she says, "That's a good thing baby, that cocaine you have is pure, it sure is better than that dirty powder coke they sell on the streets In Oakland." Her whole attitude changed, and she said, "I feel so energized right now, and don't feel depressed or stressed out about my car anymore!" Then she put a little bit more on the silver spoon and snorted again but this time she took a small snort because the coke was so good. After she finished her second blow, she took off her pants and shirt and sat next to me in her panties and bra. I was like oh shit I'm about to fuck this broad right now, but I kept my cool. I didn't come over her to hit it I came over here to secure the bag. I wanted to take this opportunity to manipulate her into going to Las Vegas with me. As calm and cool as I could be I said, "Do you still feel that you would do anything to get your car fixed?" She nonchalantly said, "The way I'm feeling about getting my car fixed right now, I would stick my head in a lion's mouth." So now I know that I have her attention I said, "Well you don't nearly have to stick your head in a lion's mouth, but some good friends of mine would stick their heads into your mouth for a thousand dollars an hour." She sobered up real quick and said, "What are you talking about?" I without blinking said, I'm talking about you dating a few tricks to help you get out of this situation you're in. Looking like I verbally assaulted her grandmother, she grabbed her heart and grasped for air, and looked at me and said, "Are you talking about the soliciting of my body for money? Again, me unflinching said, "Yeah." She got up from the couch and started walking around and said, "I don't know I'm not that type of girl, I have morals and plus I'm a college student." I felt that she was on the fence, so I decided to nudge her over it a little bit by saying, "College girls are one of the most attractive bitches who hoe, I mean women who solicit their bodies for money, plus tricks pay them the most because they know they need the money to pay for tuition and feel more comfortable around someone who is smart and who isn't going to rip them off." She stopped pacing and said, "I don't think I can stoop down that low." Then I started strategically thinking of my blackmail proposition and said, "Alright, alright, well look, how bout I get your car fixed by putting it in the shop now, and give you as much cocaine you can snort for one weekend in Las Vegas?" Nina couldn't resist, getting her car fixed, and having a free trip to Las Vegas, plus snorting all the cocaine she could snort for the entire weekend. She tilted her head to the side in a shy way and looked up at me and said, "Okay Big Dawg I'm game when do we leave?" And just like that, I found me a sexy college bitch, guess who's coming to Las Vegas?

32
CHAPTER
❖ ─────

A CRASH COURSE IN HOEING

I wanted Nina to come with me tonight while I served the late-night clientele. I wanted to school her on how to trick. She may come into contact with another pimp trying to run game on her, so I have to coach her ass up. I chilled with her in the apartment for about forty-five minutes until she finished snorting the powder coke sample that I gave her. After that, I told her to call her tow truck service and get it towed to the body shop so they could get right to it. The total for her car to be fixed was going to cost four thousand and I was going to at least get twenty-five thousand to thirty thousand out of her soliciting her body in Vegas. I was fantasizing about how much money I would make in Vegas when my phone ranged again. No worries though, it was Dee calling me for some more double up action. I said, "What's up lil brah?" Dee said, "What's up big brah? Ain't shit just pushing these rocks out here in the Wild, Wild, West we both laughed." The laughter stopped and he asked, "Are you still around, I need some more action for this four G's I got?" I'm going to always make time to get that supply to my peoples and said, "You know I got you lil brah, give me about fifteen or twenty minutes" I said. Then Dee said sarcastically, "You always say fifteen or twenty minutes even if you be an hour!" I started to laugh and responded, "Man, lil-brah I be trying to get there as quick as possible without getting pulled over by the police with all this money and dope on me. When I used to tell people, it's going to be over fifteen or twenty minutes they would tell me never mind and that they'll call somebody else and call me back when I'm not so busy. So that's why I always say that." Dee understood and said, "It's all good big brah with that good dope you sell and the double-up action you be given me, I would wait a week!" I said, "Right on Dee, I'll see you in a minute." I told Nina to put her clothes on and come with me to serve Dee so that we could spend some time together. Also, I could school her about Vegas and how to conduct herself. Nina and I arrived on the block to serve Dee his double up action for the four G's. He was shocked to see Nina instead of J.J. He got into the Expedition drooling and smiling in a daze at Nina's alluring, sexy, fine ass. I proudly gave him the eye like, "yeah nigga the bitch is fine." Trying not to stare at ole girl, he gave me the money. I could tell by the look in Nina's eyes she couldn't believe how much money that I made from one sell. She saw the dope that I handed Dee and said, "My God baby, you really are a baller!" I have never seen so much money and dope before in all of my life." I was trying not to laugh because this was one of the ways that I be showing the ladies what illegal business was worth. This is how I persuade them to do anything I wanted them to do. Lying threw my teeth I said, "Aw baby I ain't no baller, I'm trying to be a baller, that's the baller right there." I jokingly pointed to Dee, and she smiled at him with a flirtatious look and probably made his dick hard. Dee said vehemently, "Man big brah if I had your hand, I would cut mines off." In a monotone voice I said, "Everything that glitters ain't gold lil-brah, if you know what I'm saying." Nina sensing a back hand compliment punched me playfully on the arm and said, "What's that supposed to mean baby? I bet I'll be glittering when we go to Las Vegas this weekend turning them tricks for you," we both started to laugh. Dee eagerly trying to end the conversation organically says, "Alright then big brah I'm outta here, I'll catch you when you come back." He leaped out of my Expedition and went back to his place of business, and I took off driving. I was thinking of a way to kill time before someone else called and wanted to by some more from me. I decided that I would swing through mom's house to check on everybody. Nina and I got there, and my mother's car was in the driveway, along with my Big bruh's Cadillac Fleetwood Brougham parked next to it. It felt like I had been away from home for ages and was excited to see everybody. Even my dope fiend brother I was looking forward to seeing. I already prepared a fifty rock to give my second oldest brother because I knew as soon as he seen his little brother, he was going to ask for a fifty rock on credit. Nina and I walked through the front door of my mother's house. I told her to have a seat in the living room and went straight to mom's room to say hi and to give her some money. The anticipation of seeing my mother was at an all-time high, and I couldn't wait to see her. I made an entrance, "Hi mom!" She turned around and said warmly, "Hey sweetie what's going on?" I said, "Nothing much just wanted to come by and say hi." Mom got tickled and said, "Oh somebody is missing home already I see, come give momma a great big hug boy!" Of course, I obliged my mother and walked over and gave her a hug." Then I surprised her with two thousand dollars. She was showing all 62 teeth and said, "Thank you baby between you and your brother I can do the things I used to do before I retired." She said, "Shit y'all always giving me money." With gratification I proudly said, "Anything to make my mom happy." Suddenly mom looked up at me and said seriously, "You know what would really make me happy?" I was like anything for moms, what would really make you happy mom you just name it. As if she was singing a jingle and said, "If you surprised me by coming to church and worshipping the Lord with me on a Sunday." It caught me off guard and I said, "I will mom, not this Sunday but next Sunday," with a nervous smile. She just rolled her eyes and said, "You always say that every time Mommie asks you to go, next Sunday will come around and your nowhere in sight, or you'll just say not this Sunday but next Sunday, the good Lord is going to get you there one way or another, whether you go willingly or if he has to drag you by the ears!" I was beginning to sweat because I had to take that subtle tongue lashing by mom. I stood there listening to her, but I couldn't answer her back because deep down inside, I knew she was right. I could tell mom was starting to get annoyed as she brushed past me and walked into the living room. As she happens to come into the living room, she sees Nina sitting on the couch. She said, "Son you are so rude, introduce me to your company!" I introduced Nina to my mother and then she turned to continue looking at the T.V. My mom leaned into me and whispered, "That ain't Kay-Kay, how she going to feel if you brought another woman over here to meet your mother?" Without missing a beat, I answered, "Kay-Kay won't find out, and if she does, she'll get over it." Moms was trying not to make it a hostile situation while Nina was sitting there said, "Well this one show looks better than that other one I seen you with. Those clothes made her look like a prostitute." I chimed in quickly and said, "Oh that was J.J. mom." My mother feeling herself said, "You must of new better than to introduce her to me, because you know I would have had something to say!" As I lightly grabbed mom's shoulders to whisk her away in a playful manner I said, "And That's why I didn't, and I just crept on outta here ma." Finally, mom excused herself to Nina and went back to her room and closed her door. I was grateful that she left before she said something that I didn't want to be said. I sat on the couch next to her and started talking to her about what to expect from tricks and how to seduce them out of their money. The problem was that Nina was hella high off of the powder cocaine that I gave her. She didn't seem like she understood, but she nodded her head like she did. I was gaming her up on a few seductive ways to really get a tricks money. For instance, "If a trick wants some pussy, you pull your pants halfway down just to expose enough to put his dick in and if he wants you to pull your pants all the way off that's extra. Or don't take your shirt off and show your tits because if he asks to see them while he is fucking on you that's extra whatever piece of clothing, he wants you to take off its extra. I don't give a fuck if he wants you to take a dam earring off its extra. Always get the money first and act like you're calling me to let me know everything is going okay. You do that to let him know you have security, so he won't take advantage of you." Unannouncedly I was interrupted, "Big Dawg what you doing here, I thought you would be at your own apartment kicking it?" I begrudgingly turned toward the voice that was greeting me and knew it was my high ass brother. "What's up bruh what you been up to?" Surprised with my response he asked, "What I been up to, boy you miss me or something, you ain't never cared what I been up to?" he said with a smirk. Getting irritated just a little I responded, "Can't a nigga miss his brother?" Coming down from his epic high he says, "Shit Big Dawg you know what I been up to, smoking more coke than the law allows and fuckin with these difficult toss ups to get my dick sucked." I said, "Big bro yo ass is hella crazy, you ain't gone never stop." I paused and then I asked him, "Bruh just out of curiosity, how do you keep smoking coke with no job, no money, or no car?" He confidently speaks up and says with pride, "That's why I fuck with these toss-ups, that's all they is. Hoes that started smoking crack, that's how I gets high, I send them crack hoes to go get the crack while I keep the safe place in the basement for us to smoke without worrying about going to a crack house or getting busted by the police." All bitches want stability and security lil-bro, whether they crack hoes, regular hoes, or even bitches with jobs. Stability and security lil bro, and a bitch will get it." Then he said, "A brah let me holla at you in the kitchen for a minute." Knowing his routine I said, "let me guess, you want a fifty rock on credit until you hit a lick." Bruh looking surprised said, "Yeah I want a fifty on credit, but I want to talk to you about something else." We went to the kitchen, and he said, "You know that bitch you are with is high off cocaine, right?" I looked at my brother like he was another person and said, "How did you know?" He said, "Brutha, I just smoke crack I'm not stupid, I been doing this shit for years. I know when somebody is drunk, high on weed, or off heroin, especially off some powder cocaine because I used to blow that shit before I graduated to the base pipe." I said, "Yeah I know I gave her some of my coke before I cooked it up." With a serious look in his eyes my brother said to me, "lil-bro you bet not start snorting that shit or even think about it, because sometimes you can't get back right!" I reassured him, "I won't brother you just stay up." It was a slight pause and then my brother said to me, "Now give me a fifty rock!" I gave him the fifty rock and watched him disappear to the downstairs attic. I was tripping at first but then I realized… *he was a pimp too.* He's just a crack pimp. Now it's starting to make sense why I was the way I was. All of this shit is hereditary. It's like I just had this huge epiphany, and it made a lot of things seem clear to me. I would make a note to listen to what bruh had to say more than ever now. I can learn a lot from a crack pimp as much as a pimp that ain't on crack. Now I'm wondering about mom, like *did she use to be a prostitute? Was my father a pimp?* I walked back into the living room to keep giving Nina game about hoeing. That's when Big Bruh opened his door and said, "YO what you doing here boy you supposed to be at your apartment living it up like a bachelor or doing some pimpin somewhere?" I put my arms out like someone was kicking a field goal and said, "Dam a nigga can't come home and chill for a while?" With my brother's big boisterous laugh he said, "Aw boy you miss being home, we all done been through what you're going through by leaving and getting our own apartment for our privacy, we keep coming back home. Our family ties are to dam strong. Who is that in the living room?" As a proud fisherman I said, "That's the bitch I'm going to take to Vegas." As my brothers' eyes got big like golf balls he said, "Bitch! "Do you call her a bitch to her face like you do that other one?" I reassured him, Naw Big bruh, I remember what you told me about not being able to call all hoes bitches, especially if they are new to the game. Relieved he said, "I can tell by just lookin at her she is a **turn out** bitch, be careful with them turnouts because you don't know if they may get turned out by a trick. Or shit, if they get busted, they might tell the police everything they know about you to get themselves off the hook. It's so many ways the game can backfire against you when you fuckin with them turnouts. Even though we are pimps, and in the game, we still have a conscience. We don't want nothing bad to happen fuckin with any hoes we fuck with." While my brother was schooling me on the fine arts of 'turn-outs' and shit like that. I was staring at Nina while she was looking at the television and he asked, "Ay man, is that bitch off something?" I was surprised that he noticed too and said, "Dam big brah don't tell me you noticed too. Yeah, she snorts a little powder every now and then but look at how good the bitch looks." With a stern look Big Bruh answered, "lil-brah, it ain't about the beauty, it's about the duty. I want you to be careful fuckin wit that bitch, especially one on drugs." Sensing the seriousness in his voice I replied, "I will big brah I been lacing her up on what to do with the tricks and all that shit." Big Bruh said, "You gone have to lace her on way more than that if she is going to survive in the game of this pimpin and hoeing. Especially going to a cutthroat city like Las Vegas, the pimps out there are vultures, and the bitches out there are sharks!" I had to interrupt him because he was starting to get riled up and said, "I got it all under control Big Bruh." Acting as if he was reliving something personal that happened to him. Big Bruh went to the kitchen and then went back to his room with ambivalence. I said goodbye to moms, and my brothers, and Nina and I headed out the door. I wandered why I haven't heard from Kay-Kay all day. I figured she must be busy with Boo and getting the rest of my money. It seemed like once a customer calls, then everybody starts calling me all at the same time. I was busy serving customers and talking about Las Vegas that I didn't finish schooling Nina about the game anymore, hell I got busy. When night was up, we went back to our apartment to shut it down for the rest of the night. I parked my truck in the stall and gave her some more powder to snort on and walked her to the doorstep. She said, "Thank you for helping me get my car fixed and being a good friend consoling me through my ruff times. I'll show you how much it means to me when we get down to Las Vegas and I turn these tricks for you." Shaking my head in agreement I said, "I know you will baby, just be ready to go down there and use your hips, lips, and fingertips, so we can come up!" She opened her door with her key to the noise of her roommates partying at it once again. When she stepped inside, I heard her say, "look what I got y'all" closing the door behind her.

33

CHAPTER

❖

GAME ON GAME OVER

A few days had passed, and it was time to go to Sin City. I still haven't heard from Kay-Kay or J.J. for that matter. For some reason, I really didn't care because I was juiced that I was on my way to Las Vegas. The fact that I persuaded a pretty, sexy, bad, thick, looking bitch to sale her body for me while I was down there. I got my clothes out the cleaners, packed some outfits and was ready to go. Nina got her hair done, and her hands manicured, and feet pedicured. She was ready to leave as well, and you could feel the excitement and nervousness from her. We rode on the Freeway for about 8 hours and saw the light from the Excalibur Casino beaming into the sky letting us know that we have arrived in "Sin City". Once we were on the Strip, I pulled into a casino so we could get ourselves checked in and situated. It was prime time when we arrived. Everything was at full swing and there was no time to be wasting. Nina got herself dressed up looking like one of Vegas's finest. We left the casino and were walking down the Strip. I turned to her and said, "O.K. baby this is it! I'm going to stand either across the street or behind you and talk to you on your cellphone and tell you were to go and what to do. Once you think you have a potential costumer hang up the phone and do your thing. I want you to charge one thousand dollars an hour off the top and remember everything else is extra." She was rubbing her hands together like she was getting ready to kick some ass and said, "O.K. baby I'm a little nervous but I'm ready." Like a cornerman talking to his boxer in the corner I said, "That's alright baby its natural for you to be nervous your first-time turning tricks, but once you make a few thousand dollars those butterflies in your stomach will fly away and you will be ready to get money all night." Here is a little something to help them go away." I handed her a baggie full of powder coke. Her eyes light up like a Rockefeller Christmas tree on Christmas day.

She tucked the powder in her bra and told me she would see me later. As she walked on the Strip in Las Vegas all kinds of men were getting at her. Some were regular dudes that wanted to have fun, and some were actual tricks seeing how much she charged and if she had a room already. After about forty-five minutes she finally landed her first trick. She did everything I coached her to do. She came back from her first tricks hotel in less than thirty minutes with sixteen hundred dollars on her. She called me and we met at a secluded area so she could give me the money. When she saw me, she said, "Baby I did it I did it! I got sixteen hundred dollars and all I had to do was let him jack off on my titties, she was excited and happy that things went smoothly so quick. As I was reaching out to collect my dough I said, "See baby I told you it would be okay, I bet you don't feel those butterflies in your stomach now." She is pacing back and forth with adrenaline flowing and said, "What butterflies? shit I'm ready to go back out there and get some more money!" I told her that's what's up and said, "Alright baby same routine." She headed back on the Strip while I walked behind her coaching her over the phone. She got another date and this time she made three thousand for 2 and a half hours. She had to do way more than she did the first time but didn't mind because she thought the trick was cute. We did this all night until 6 am in the morning. I took Nina to a restaurant so that we could eat breakfast and get some rest. We had to be ready for prime time later that evening. I counted fifteen thousand dollars and some change and let her know that she was doing a hell of a job. She was happy she could help me the way I helped her. Her ass was still wide awake and alert, from all that powder coke she was snorting. Lastly, we took it on inside the hotel to get some sleep and energy to hit the track hard for later. As we finally awaken from our slumber, we both showered and got dressed and hit the town. It was about 9 pm when we got on the Strip of Las Vegas, and I said, "Baby do you think you still need me to be across the street or behind you to help you get this money?" Eager to get out there again she said, "No baby I'm a big girl now I can handle myself out there!" Feeling her confidence I said, "O.K. well I'm going to go to the crap tables and see if I can win a few thousand dollars with the money we made so far." She shrugged it off and said, "Go ahead I will call you and let you know every time I get a trick. I'll let you know where I'm at, so you don't have to worry." Licking my lips I said, "Cool baby." She sashayed her body on down the boulevard, while I went inside one of the casinos. I looked older than I really was, so I didn't have to worry about someone asking me for I.D. I walked through the casino and saw a lot of people spending big money, and they were dressed to impress. I was excited by the glitz and glamour my dam self. It's hard to believe that back in the day mobsters made this 'adult' Disneyland for grownups. I fucking love it! I pulled up to a crap table that was crowded with hella players. I watched and observed to see how the game was played then the stick man put the dice in front of me unexpectedly and asked if I waited to shoot. I ain't no punk so I'm about to handle mines you feel me? Right when I was about to pick up the dice my dam cellphone rings. It was Nina and I had to answer it. I excused myself from the table and answered, "What's up baby?" Sounding like she just caught a fish while fishing, "I got another date baby I will be two hotels from where you are gambling at." Proudly I said, "Alright babe you know what to do, get that money!" She said, "I will, and I'll call you after I'm done." I hung up the phone and readied myself at the table and picked up the dice. I said, "Fuck it" and pulled out a Gee and placed a hundred dollars' worth of bets on the table. I talked to the dice as I shook them. I cocked my hand back and hit seven on the first roll and collected my monies. Of course, I'm feeling myself; I have strangers high fiving me because of my roll, they all won. I decided I was going to take a bigger chance and placed three hundred dollars' worth of bets and rolled the dice. After about four rolls I hit my point and won again after about forty-five minutes. Nina called again I had stopped in mid stroke to answer the phone. Sounding like she is trying to top her personal best she said, "I got you thirteen hundred baby." I cracked a smile and said, "Alright keep doing what you're doing and call me back." Now, I'm getting back to my dice game and when I proceeded to roll the dice… I crapped out. I was a little upset thinking I shouldn't have answered my phone in mid stroke because it cooled me off. After about 5 more calls from Nina in about 3 hours' worth of time, the dice was back on me. This time I wasn't going to answer when she called me if I was on a good roll. I placed my bets and got back hot again. I hit my point four times in a row I was on fire, then my phone ranged again. I didn't answer and kept on shooting dice after I crapped out… I called Nina. I called her back hoping that everything is good and asked, "What's up baby?" Sounding like a kid who just saw the "ice cream man" she says, "Guess what baby, I met another girl out her working and she said she knows where we can find tricks coming from a club not too far from here. Do you think it's a good idea if I go with her?" I was glad she had somebody to hoe with because now, I could concentrate on rolling dice and wouldn't have to tend to her every call. I responded, "Yeah baby go ahead, how much money have you made so far?" She said, "I got sixty-five hundred on me and it's still pretty early, I even have some powder left over from last night, so I should be okay." Approving her new move I said, "Hit me later on then when your finished getting money with your new friend." Sounding like a little kid being told that she can go outside she happily said, "O.K.!" Taking this hoeing to heart, she and her new hoe friend went to the club where the so-called tricks were at. Nina and the new hoe were at the club doing **their thang** when suddenly the new hoe says, "Hey girlfriend I gots to go home and change clothes, do mind coming with me? Looking like the wolf who was trying to eat red riding hood and said, "When I'm finished changing clothes we can come back." Not thinking clearly Nina said, "Sure I want to take a break for a little bit anyway." They left the club and got into the cab and took all kinds of back roads and turns. They finally arrived at the hoe friend's house.

They walked for about five minutes before they came to her doorstep. When they walked inside a man was sitting on the couch in some slacks, sandals, and a wife beater. She couldn't really see his face due to all of the smoke in there, but she could tell that he was an older black dude. The new hoe friend introduced the man as her pimp and went to act as if she was changing clothes. The new hoes pimp was being nice to Nina and asked her if she wanted to be on his team. She politely refused and said that she was happy with who she was dealing with and told him no thank you. The new hoes pimp was furious and decided to deceive her as best as he could. He went to where his hoe was changing clothes and came back and asked Nina, if she wanted a drink. Not thinking clearly, she accepted the drink and drank it all up. The drink went down smooth even though it tasted kind of funny. She thought maybe she had just been snorting too much coke and paid it no attention. After about thirty minutes, her new hoe friend asked her to come into the bathroom with her. As soon as she stood up, she got dizzy and almost stumbled over. Finally, she got on her own two feet but unaware she left her purse in the living room with the new hoes pimp. Soon as she was in the bathroom, the new hoes pimp went through Nina's purse and found the six thousand and five that she was supposed to give me. When the women came out of the bathroom the new hoes pimp nodded at her and gave her the approval of the scandal he had just done. The new friend hoe said, "Nina let's get you back to the club so we can have fun and make some more money." She responded with a slow incoherent "O…k" as if she was in space. They got back in the cab and took back streets and all kinds of turns again. Once back at the club Nina's new how friend had ditched her in the club and got back into a cab and went back home. She was still trying to get some dates when she noticed she didn't see her friend. She was dizzier than she was when she first left her hoe friend's apartment. Teetering back and forth, she fell out into the middle of the club. After she blacked out for about 6 hours, she was awakened in the back of the club. The owners crowded around her asking if she was alright? She said, "I'm alright and maybe I just had too much to drink." As she called me, I answered saying, "Hey babe are you making money and having fun?" I could tell she was groggy and said, "No baby something bad has happened, my new hoe friend persuaded me to go to her house and she brought me to her pimp, and he tried to get me to be on his team. When I said No, he offered me a drink and I drank it. I haven't been feeling good ever since. My hoe friend ditched me at the club, then I blacked out in the middle of the dance floor." Fearing that all of that money is gone I calmly said, "Alright baby catch a cab back to where I am," I don't know where you are." Nina said in a hysterical voice, "And I don't know where I am, baby I'm scared!" I had to think quick and said, "Calm down baby just calm down, ask the club owners where you are and how to get back to the Las Vegas Strip and I will meet you at the lobby of our hotel!" But due to being out for so long she didn't remember shit! She said, "I don't remember the hotel baby I don't remember anything." I'm like fuck! Then I said, "Tell the cab to take you to the Piper hotel on the Las Vegas Strip and I will be outside waiting." She drowsily said, "O…. K." When she got to the hotel about 1 hour after talking to me, she reached in her purse to get some money to pay the cab driver and discovered her money was gone. I ran to the cab a noticed she was crying, and she said that the money she had for me was gone. I was hella mad as I paid the cab driver and we both went inside the hotel. The first thing that came to my head was what my brother told me was that the pimps are vultures, and the hoes are sharks. After she told me the story again, I knew that her new hoe friends' pimp had put a **mickey** in her fucking drink. She was upset because the money was gone and how she got played like a fool. I didn't want to tell her that she got a **mickey** put in her drink and told her to forget about the money and that things could've been worse. From that day on Nina was never the same because of what that Vegas pimp put in her drink. What happened to her is a bitter pill for me to swallow because truth be told, it was all my fault. I should've protected her more and If I had not been so hung up on that crap game, we would've been cool. As a matter of fact, I didn't come up here to Vegas to fucking throw dice anyway. I came out here to get paid, and for a moment I took my eyes off the prize. If I had coached her more and by staying behind her or across the street. I should've picked up the money when she first said she had it. If I had not let her go with some hoe friend nobody knew anything about, this wouldn't have happened. After that last my spirits were crushed. I felt that I failed as a pimp on my first trip to Las Vegas. As we were riding in the car, her that she didn't have to worry about making any more money while we were here and to just eat, rest, and enjoy herself. My fucking conscience was eating me up because of what I did by manipulating her to solicit her body for me and money. On our way back home on the Freeway she was in a deep sleep like she was in a comma. She never shook off whatever it was that fucked her up. Months later she had to move back home with her parents because she wasn't making the cut at school. That one is on me. I was driving around reflecting on the life and how I'm living. I thought dam what am I becoming? I sell drugs and now I'm a pimp. Do drug dealers and pimps go through what I'm going through? My friend Dave-baby got killed, J.J. got caught up snorting heroin from some trick, plus she went to jail fucking with me. Kay-Kay is so infatuated by me she gets the shit beat out of her just to pay me. My brother is a straight up crackhead pimp, and the other one is a full pledge 100% pimp. I have no woman I can call my own. No real friends and I just manipulated someone into soliciting her body for me and she will never be the same. Who knows the long term affect that it might have on her later down the road? I got robbed, I almost got killed from some jealous jay cats I don't even know. I'm not sure what is going to happen to me next. Whatever it is I can't worry about it because for some reason, I love this life, I'm loving the cars, clothes, money and hoes. I can't seem to stop wanting more. Maybe I need to concentrate more on my trucking business and going legit. I will, once I get enough money to buy a big rig and 2 trailers. Doing the calculations that shit is going to cost me about two thousand dollars. I should be close to at least one hundred and twenty thousand with what I got on me. Plus, the money and dope I have saved at Kay-Kay's house. All I need is eighty thousand dollars, and I can kick back. Yeah, so that's what I'll do just get the eighty thousand and go legit. Or so I thought.

34
CHAPTER
❖
THE BRIDGE IS OVER

When I got back to the Bay area, I forgot all about what I thought of doing on the way back from Vegas. My alter ego kicked in, and all I wanted was to find another hoe I could take to Las Vegas and make it my place of residence. I needed a change of scenery and was getting tired of selling dope. I was tired of dealing with the headache of cooking coke, bagging it up, trying not to get caught with it, and everything else that came with it. Now that I have a taste of pimping, I feel that pimping was way safer and almost just as lucrative. I had the game on how to pimp a female to get paid. I just needed one or two that didn't use drugs and that was the hard part. I needed a bitch that had some class and a head on her shoulders. I dropped Nina off at home and thanked her for helping a brutha out. I let her know that her car would be ready in a few days. I reminded her that it was already paid for. I gave her another baggie of powder cocaine and took myself to my apartment. I was thinking, *dam where can I find me some more hoes?* I went to sleep, deep in thought about that subject on my mind. I woke up later on the next day with that same thought in my head. It was about 10:30am so I decided to call up my pimp buddy I met in San Francisco. I wanted to pick his brain to see if he knew where I could scout out some potential hoes as opposed to the ones on the track. The pimp said, "Hey young pimpin what's going on with you?" I responded, "Just another one, like the other one." After all of the pleasantries I said, "Say pimp I'm trying to figure out something, where can I find some reputable hoes who might want to fuck with some of this pimpin I got for them?" The pimp laughed and adjusted his clothes and said, "Oh so you on one of those missions huh? trying to look for a bitch in the daytime with a flashlight huh? Well, when you are on one of those you can always hit the Strip clubs, malls, escort services, or even get on the Internet and search the websites." He was making things look clearer and I said, "Shit why didn't I think about that, I could've been at least hitting a few different Strip clubs to come up on a bitch or two." But why would I call the escort services? The pimp let out a blustery laugh and you could tell his head was back and said, "Because young pimpin, you can have a hoe delivered to your doorstep, it's up to you what to say and do in order to knock the bitch. I've done that on several occasions." Innocently I said, "But that would be wasting the hoes time and the service though, right?" Suddenly the pimp stops laughing and said in a stern voice, "So what young pimpin, it ain't like it's costing you nothing and when it comes to knocking a hoe all is fair game. Even if you have to act like you're a trick to get the hoe in your presence. If the bitch wasn't sharp enough not to tell the difference, then that's on her. Her pimp or the escort service that sent the bitch to you is all fair game. All she can do is get away from your pimpin or run to it, just remember to always conduct yourself as a gentleman. He continues, "Don't ever do no desperate pimpin where you need a hoe so bad you kidnap her or pimp on a minor because that shit ain't cool." With confirmation I said, "Dam pimp, this shit ain't as easy as I thought it was." The pimp erupted before he took a sip of his drink and said, "Hell naw it ain't easy, it just looks like it is!" He continued, "But once you get a good stable of hoes with some brains it can be a success. So don't get discouraged it ain't gone happen overnight, plus you have to stay pimpin at a bitch 24-7 you have to act as if you are broke and have no ends even when things are going cool." Feeling like the end of class I said, "Thanks pimp for helping me once again broaden my horizons. let me get back to you a little later I got some traps to check and a whole lot of pimpin to do." While fixing his clothes the pimp says in conclusion, "Stay down young pimpin, and hit me whenever you need me." As I hung up the phone I said, "4 show." I was wondering why Kay-Kay hasn't called me in the last couple of days because that ain't like her. I was also tripping off why I haven't heard from J.J. since I gave her that five hundred dollars when she got out of jail. Hoping for the best, but expecting the worse, I called Kay-Kay's number and her phone was disconnected. I hurried up and dialed again to make sure that I called the right number. I got the same results. Starting to think that maybe *Kay-Kay forgot to pay her bill and that she would pay it as soon as she noticed her phone wasn't working.* As much as she likes to talk on the phone, I know that would be soon. Alright moving right along I called J.J. cellphone number but didn't get an answer either. So, I left her a message thinking maybe she was asleep. I got up and showered, shaved, then got myself dressed in some Stacey Adams, Enyce jeans, and a Coogi sweater. I sprayed on some smell good and was ready to find me some more hoes to be down with me. By the time I got into my car and left the bachelor's pad in Hayward heading towards Oakland, it was about 12:30pm. It had been two hours since I had last called Kay-Kay and J.J. I decided to call J.J.'s phone first this time, and still got no answer. Right when I was about to call Kay-Kay, Dee called me. He said, "What's up big brah what you been into?" Glad to hear his voice I said, "What's up Dee I just got back from Vegas last night and boy was the road bumpy." Not sounding phased by what I just said he responded, "Ay big brah I got some money I want to spend with you, the usual four G's plus I want to show you something I think you might want to see." With my interest being peaked I said, "Alright, I'll see you in fifteen or twenty minutes at our same meeting spot." While I'm driving to the meeting spot I called Kay-Kay and still her line was disconnected. So now I'm like fuck it, and I decided to call J.J.'s home phone number. It was the first number she had given me when we first met at the nail shop. A sensual voice answered, "Hello?" I said, "Hi may I speak with J.J.?" The voice said, "Who is this, Big Dawg?" I laughed and said, "Yeah this is me who is this?" Responding back to me with a slight attitude she says, "This is Karen J.J.'s older sister do you remember me?" I quickly responded, "How could I forget such a woman as pretty as you, of course I remember you?" Over the phone I could hear her smiling and she said, "Thank you for the compliment you just made my day." But turning serious she said, "J.J. hasn't been home in a few days, the last I heard she was with you. I thought maybe you guys went out of town to get some money or something. She hasn't been answering her phone, plus I noticed she has been acting funny lately." Reassuring her I said, "I dropped her off at home a few days ago and gave her $500 hundred dollars to do something nice for herself. I hope nothing has happened to her." Sarcastically she quipped, "See that's what happens when you fuck around with them young hoes. They aren't experienced enough when it comes to dealing with money and having tricks. You need an older hoe like me so you can have a stable and don't have to be worrying about babysitting bitches and keeping track of them. All you need to do is peel money, touch bitches, and kick back and count your riches if you know what I'm saying?" I'm contemplating about putting her on the team as well and I responded, "I'll keep that in mind pretty lady but first let me see if I can find your sister to at least make sure she is okay." With her final parting shot she said, "I'm not choosing baby I'm just trying to make it easier on the young pimpin with so much potential. let me know when you find her so that I'll know she is okay too." Reassuring her again I sternly said, "I got chew" and then we hung up. I made it to the spot where me and Dee usually meet to do our drug transaction in fifteen minutes on the dot. I was curious about what he wanted to show me. I was eager to get the rest of those bundles he had on him too. I can't wait to get these bundles off me so I would have a reason to stop by Kay-Kay's house to cook and bag up the rest of the dope. Dee got into my Expedition; we did our 'exchange.' He told me to drive him up the street where he sells his dope in West Oakland. His mood was kind of somber and he was acting like this, I had to see. He told me to "Park right here." He asked me to follow him up into this knocks house that he be serving. I never had the feeling that it was a setup, or else I would've taken my strap with me. I got out of the truck and followed Dee up the stairs to the knocks house. He opened the door like he was trying to surprise some cockroaches and said scathingly, "look and pointed!" What I saw I couldn't believe my eyes. I saw J.J. with a base pipe in her mouth lighting up some crack on the top of the screen. She had on the same funky clothes she had worn when I had bailed her out of jail just before I left for Vegas. I kept my cool like a gentleman is supposed to and asked solemnly, "How long has she been her Dee?" He turned to me with an even more somber look and said, "She been here for about four or five days big brah, she came spending some big cheese maybe up to about five hundred dollars. Then when that was all gone, she started sucking mothafuckas dicks for a hit of some crack. I found out because a knock had told me they had a young cute bitch in the house sucking dick, for dime pieces. I was like cool because I had wanted my dick sucked right quick while I was out here getting my money. I went inside the house and saw it was the bitch you always had with you riding in the front seat when you be coming to serve me." I crossed my arms with my head tilted and said, "So what did you do Dee?" He nervously stepped back and adjusted his shirt and said, "Shit, I got my dick sucked from the bitch!" I waited for you to come back from Vegas so I can give you a heads up on what the bitch was up to." I looked at Dee and grinned and said, "Boy you know that bitch sucked you so good she almost suck one of those G bundles out yo ass!" Laughing hysterically Dee said, "I ain't gone lie big brah, the bitch had me coming back like a junkie on heroin. She got me for at least six hundred in dope plus a few dollars. We both started laughing in a whispering tone then I said, "Well the bridge is over, and this was her last stop with me, but I want you to do me favor." His body language stiffened up and he responded, "Anything big brah just name it." I spoke firmly and said, "I want you to watch over her for me as best as you can. If you can, make sure nothing happens to her. She's a young bitch, maybe when she gets back to her usual self, she can go through one of those rehabs or something and get her life back together." Appearing to be patriotic Dee announced, "You got that big brah I'll watch over her. I'll watch over her like a correctional officer watch over convicts at chow time to make sure that nothing goes down." With that being said, I stepped inside the room just enough so that J.J. could see me. Her attention was momentarily diverted from hitting the pipe when she looked up at me. But after long the pipe called her back and she proceeded to give in to the urge. She shed two tears down the cheeks of her cute face and begin to light the crack that was on the screen of the pipe. After we caught eye contact for about 10 long seconds, I blew her a kiss and tapped my chin with the opposite side of my hand telling her to keep her head up then closed the door. Shaking my head as if I just left her funeral, I jumped back into the Expedition and headed towards Kay-Kay's house so I could check on my stash and handle my business.

35
CHAPTER
❖
ENTER DIAMONDS

As I drove away, I pondered how J.J. got hooked on crack. *Maybe it happened that one time we were in the hood, and she went and started hoeing on E 14th with the rest of the crackhead hoes. She probably did that shit while I was selling dope down the street.* Either way it went I knew one thing for sure and two things for certain. That's one of the reasons why pimps don't fall in love with hoes because you never know what they will turn out to be or what will happen to them. I also understand why pimps kept hoes broke, because if you give them some dam money to splurge, they are subject to go crazy. I needed to make sure that shit never happens to me again and stay on top of my game by all means. I ain't gone front I chuckled to myself thinking about how *J.J. was sucking Dee out of his sack.* I'm already knowing how J.J. gets down and Dee better watch out or she'll turn him into somebody like my brother. I remembered him telling me that a bitch turned him out on crack. He said that it was because, he was weak for her, and he thought she was so fine. finally, I arrived at Kay-Kay's house, the first thing I peeped was that her car was not in the driveway like normally. I figured she went to go pay her phone bill realizing it was off, so I parked the SUV and got out. As I was walking towards Kay-Kay's house, I looked at her windows and for some odd reason they looked empty. While staring at the window, and walking up the stairs to her house, I suddenly had this realization of why the windows looked so empty. The curtains that usually hanged were gone. With my heart racing, I tripped trying to get up the stairs to quickly. Approaching the front screen door, it was unlocked and looked empty inside. The wooden door was kind of off the hinges and was halfway open leaning to the side. Now worry raced through my mind like *did her house get raided? Did some jealous ass niggas raid her shit, and they took everything? As a matter of fact, where in the fuck is she and how come I ain't heard nothing from the homies?* Trying to brace myself for what I might find, I stepped through the front door and gasped in shock with my mouth hung to the ground. I stared at an empty house that looked like a soul never even lived in there. Hurrying up and checking Kay-Kay's room for my stash immediately I realized that shit was empty. I checked the kitchen, empty. My head felt like it was swirling around because I was so astonished at what I saw that I couldn't even think straight! Kay-Kay getting me for all my money and dope was the last thing on my mind! This bitch just signed her death warrant. After a while I settled down and thought well dam what happened? Then I thought that *somebody dropped a dime and informed the police. They probably came and kicked the door in and found the money, drugs, and seized all Kay-Kay's possessions thinking it belonged to her.* Fuck it, I called the Oakland Police department to see if they had her in custody. To my relief they didn't have her in custody and had never heard of her. That was good news but now I'm thinking did she just run off with my shit? She had enough money, and I haven't been here for a least a week. I thought that *maybe somebody kicked the door in and robbed her and got all the money and dope.* But why wouldn't she be here or not have called me, and who would've robbed somebody for money and dope and then take the time to still the furniture too? It would've had to be some bold muthafucka's or some desperate dope fiends. I started putting two and two together then sat in the middle of the living room on the floor and said, "Dam, Kay-Kay got me!" Sitting there in the middle of the living room for about fifteen minutes in disbelief, shock, and depression. I got my shit together, now vengeance, anger, and revenge, took over the feeling I had about fifteen minutes ago. Getting up off the living room floor I stomped my way back to the car. I had no idea where I should start looking for Kay-Kay first. I decided that the best thing to do would be to wait till something turned up. She would defiantly slip up and something would leak out from somewhere or somebody. Now that this new development has happened, I only had a little over thousand dollars left from the time I left for Vegas and came back. With Kay-Kay stealing from me, my hoe J.J. on crack, Nina being slipped a **mickey**, Dave-baby dead, the turf being hot, I have no source of income right now! A whole bunch of doubt is racing across my mind and I'm thinking, *will I ever be able to get two hundred thousand for my own trucking company?* I pondered how many obstacles am I going to have to hurdle over to get to the top? Is this game for me? Should I just say fuck it and throw in the towel? Should I go to church like my mom said? As I drove back to my apartment in Hayward my alter ego kicked in. The words blurted out of me like an alcoholic that had enough to drink and threw up and said, "Fuck Naw!" I ain't about to throw in no dam towel. The harder I fall the quicker I come back up, that's what makes me a real nigga in this game. I said defiantly trying to rally myself back up. Now I'm pointing my index finger at an imaginary person straight up in their face and saying, "I'm going to knock me some hoes and move my ass to Las Vegas and win!" I pulled into my apartment complex and regrouped my thoughts. Getting dressed up in my most flashy and flamboyant outfit that I could think of and headed out to the Strip club in San Francisco. I was on a mission in search of a hoe that I could find to manipulate to be down with me to go to Las Vegas. The first time I went in hot pursuit of a new prostitute I came up with nothing. The next night the second time nothing, the third as the same as the first nothing. I was starting to get frustrated because I did this for 2 weeks straight! Bingo! I knocked me a pretty cute 5-foot 4 brown skinned bitch with a nice body, long hair and titties and ass to match. She had a cute face, but her eyes and eyebrows were dangerous. You could tell she was fed up with the world shitting on her and she was ready to let you know about it. This was her 8th time seeing me come through the Strip club. She admired me for my determination to get what I wanted. She would've hollered when she first saw me, but I was talking to every bitch in the club. When I caught her looking at me, I motioned for her to come here. Looking and walking alluring towards me she asks, "Do you want a lap dance?" With my head tilted to the side and a toothpick in my mouth I said, "Baby you been seeing me here for the past week or two and you know I don't want no dam lap dance. What I do want is a bitch that's compatible with me in adventure with confidence, class, and personality. Someone that's nice young and down to ride, by a pimp's side." After I hollered at her I cracked my million-dollar smile and extended my hand for her to shake it not giving her an option to say no. I introduced myself and she said that her name is Diamond. She shook my hand and I held hers and pulled her closer to me and whispered in her ear, "Come on get your shit and let's leave, I'm going to take you to the land of milk and honey were it ain't bout nothing but the money." The stripper girl was already infatuated with my determination. Now she was infatuated (times 3) by my assertiveness, appearance, and my language. All she could say was, "Let me go to my locker and get my things and I will be ready in 10 minutes." And just like that, I had me a bitch that I could go back to Las Vegas with.

36
CHAPTER
❖
RETRAINING A BITCH

Her name is Diamond, and I spent the next week or so getting acquainted to her. I had to gain her trust by showing her the type of gentleman I was. At times I would call her a bitch to see what type of reaction I would from her. She wasn't tripping and didn't seem to mind. Starting her training, I made it a habit by calling her a bitch like I did J.J. The only difference is I would do it by being smooth and not calling her a bitch in vain. As I was wooing her and getting to know her, I learned that she came from a small family that had no money. She has a recovering addict as a mother, and a father nowhere to be found. She also told me that she had a son from a no-good baby daddy who she would always get into fights with. One day, she came over to my apartment and cooked dinner, cleaned the house, and stayed watching movies with me until 4 a.m. I thought she was about to stay all night, so I wasn't tripping and then she said she was about to go home. I was curious so I asked, "How did you get here and how are you getting home?" She said, "Oh my mother is outside waiting in the car." I looked at her with an expression of disbelief and said, "Your mother was outside waiting on you all this time? Why didn't you tell me? I wouldn't have had you stay so late if I would have known?" Then she said in a spiteful tone, "Fuck that bitch, she can stay her ass in the car all night for all I care." I said, "Diamond that's hella rude and why are you referring to your mother like that?" With her scathing response she says, "Shit baby, fuck her ass I don't care if she is waiting in her car." I had to see this for myself, so I went outside to discover a middle-aged pretty light skinned lady asleep in her car with the radio on. I knocked on the window lightly not to surprise her and said, "Excuse me ma'am are you Diamond's mother?" While yarning she said, "Yes I am." With sincerity I stated, "I'm so sorry ma'am, I had no idea that you gave her a ride here and she left you sitting in the car. If I had known that I would've invited, you inside to eat and watch a few movies with us." With the upmost respect for her mom because, I was raised with respect and home training you feel me? "Then she said, "Thank you but I don't think Diamond would've wanted me in the house with you guys because she says I'm embarrassing." I was appalled and said, "I don't care what she says, this is my house and I have respect for my elders. So come on in and make yourself comfortable and get you something to eat." As she was getting out of the car Diamond's mom felt that her daughter had finally gotten herself a real gentleman. Her mom was thinking because any other dude would've let her sit in the car and had no hospitality. Her mother was four eleven, hella light skinned possibly Creo, overweight, beautiful green eyes, good hair in a frazzled ponytail. She wore a mint green old looking sweatsuit, with a dingy white tee shirt. When her mom came into the house Diamond instantly rolled her eyes at her mom and mom stuck her tongue out at her. Not amused but rather irritated Diamond said, "See baby this old ungrateful bitch doesn't even appreciate the fact that you let her in your house! That's because she has no life, no man, or nowhere to go." I looked upside her head and said, "She ain't did nothing to me to show she don't appreciate it. All she did was tell me Thank you. I think it's **you** that has the problem not appreciating your mom." Diamonds mom said innocently, "Thank you Sir, she always treats me like this. She is the evilest thing in the world when it come to her mother. I don't know where she gets it from and why." I was light weight thinking *maybe her mom and her are trying to con me or rob me.* Just then my thoughts get interrupted with Diamond screaming, "Bitch shut yo punk ass up, I hate yo muthafuckin ass I swear I wish you would disappear or die and just get the fuck out of my life!" So now I flashed and said, "Bitch you shut up before I slap the shit out of yo ass for talking to your mother like that in front of me." I didn't know where my actions came from, but I had a feeling that dealing with Diamond wasn't going to be easy. She has a foul mouth and too erratic. I'm not going to let that stop me from taking her to Vegas. I told her to shut up, she kept on talking to her mother in the most disrespectful way I that I have heard of. Before I knew it, I slapped the dog shit out of her ass. Her mother smirked with a grin of approval to me, and Diamond shut the fuck up quick. Then she said, "I'm sorry daddy" to me and I said, "Bitch don't say sorry to me say it to your mother!" She then turned to her mother and apologized. I was in shock of how a slap in the face solved the situation and how obedient she was after that. I never had to put hands on Kay-Kay, J.J., Sasha, or Nina. Acting and sounding all docile she said, "Daddy I'm tired is it okay if me and my mother spend the night with you?" Without hesitation I said, "Yeah it's cool" then I just remembered something and asked, "Where is your baby?" She replied, "He is with his auntie my mother's sister." My auntie doesn't allow for me and my mother to stay there even though we have no place to stay. She just lets the baby stay there because she says that the baby shouldn't have to sleep in cars and in different hotels. My auntie says that because me and my momma ain't got our shit together." Then I asked, "Why don't you and your momma have a place to stay?" Embarrassed she responded, "We got evicted out of our last apartment because my mother spent all of her money on that dam car, she got out there." Not judging but I said, "Well why didn't you hold it down until she got back on her feet? You are working at that Strip Club you should've made more than enough money to pay the rent and all the bills." Trying to save face she says, "Because daddy she is supposed to be a grandmother and a mother and handle her responsibilities like one. Plus, I needed my money to do what I wanted to do." So now I'm curious and thinking like what?" She trying to think fast and stated, "like get my nails did, my hair, some clothes, and go to the club and kick it with my friends." I'm standing there appalled and asked, "You don't buy your baby nothing?" Nonchalantly she shrugged her shoulders and said, "My auntie by that lil nigga shit." I was in shock when she referred to her son as a 'little nigga.' Now I see why they don't have shit; they need a dam manager. I told her you never put that bullshit before your priorities." I knew that fuckin with Diamond and her family wasn't worth it, but I had no other way to make any money right now and I needed to go back to Vegas bad. I told Diamond's mom she could sleep on the couch, and I gave her some covers to keep herself warm. I respectfully motioned for Diamond to follow me to the bedroom so that we can go to sleep. When we laid down, I yelled to her mom, "What's your name mam?" and she yelled back "Christy!" I awoke in my California king size bed with the sight of Diamond sucking on my dick. She was doing it like a pro and talking to me at the same time. I had to build up the strength to push her away because that was one of my ways of controlling her. I mastered and manipulated these bitches by not letting a bitch suck my dick. I don't let them suck or fuck me until I felt the funds were sufficient and they passed the hoe prospecting period. She asked with spit and slob on her mouth, "Daddy did I do something wrong?" Acting unfazed I replied, "Hell yeah you did something wrong bitch. You ain't gave me nowhere near enough money or passed my hoe probation to be sucking on my dick. Get yo ass the fuck from by me before I slap the shit out of your ass like I did last night!" I was going to treat her like shit because she deserved it. The way she treats her mom and don't take care of her kid fuck her! Looking confused she said, "I'm sorry daddy I just wanted to make you feel good." I barked back, "Bitch that ain't how you make me feel good, if you want to make me feel good, start cleaning up this house and cook me some food." She acquiesced and spoke softly, "Okay daddy, I'm going to start right now," and cleaned up herself. I was surprised how she was so submissive. She wasn't like any of the other ladies that I had dealt with before, but she came with a lot of baggage. I made myself a promise, and that promise is for me to work with her on being respectful toward her mother, and to take care of her baby before it was all over. I went in the living room to see Christy Diamond's mom laid out on the couch snoring with her mouth wide open. I could tell by how deep her sleep was that she hadn't gotten any real sleep for a while. As I moved silently through the living room, I noticed Christy had brought some bags of clothes from her car. She also had a bunch of women products like she was going to be here for a while. I just had a funny feeling about fuckin with Diamond and all this baggage she came with. The glitz and glamour of Las Vegas flushed through my head and erased the problems that she came with. Silently Diamond walked in the living room behind me and said in an rancorous whisper tone, "See daddy look at this bitch, she all on your couch snoring hella loud and, the bitch looks like she is enjoying it." She looked on the floor and saw her mother's bags and feminine products and asked, "What the hell is that?" Me not tripping off her said, "I don't know, she must've gone to the car and got some of her stuff last night." With a jealous undertone she said, "Hell naw daddy, that bitch think she is about to be here for a while and didn't even see if it was OK!" "Shhh" I said, "You are going to wake her." I was contemplating that maybe her being here for a while could be put to good use. Looking incredulous she asked, "How?" Calmly I said, "She can start by going to get your baby from your aunt's house so y'all can start spending quality time with him. She softened her stance and smiled at me for having compassion toward her son. Deep down inside she was happy I was showing compassion for her mom as well. Newly motivated she covertly asked, "Daddy when are we going to Las Vegas?" Unemotionally I answered, "In a couple of days bitch. My long-term goal really is to move down there so I can do some pimpin and start this trucking company up that I've been wanting to do. I almost had enough money to do it, but I ran into some obstacles to stagnate my progress. Bringing my attention back to her I said, "We will go down there and see how you do, and if you do good then I will move down there, and you can come with me." As I told her she can come with me, her face lit up and she was filled with Joy. She started jumping up and down and felt like she had finally found her prince charming. Suddenly, we heard "What's going on? Why are you so happy Diamond? Her mother said waking up from a deep sleep. Her happiness turned upside down into a frown and said, "Nothing, you need to get up, get yo shit and leave!" I turned around at her and said angrily, "Diamond what did I just say?" then she said, "Momma you lucky he wants to help us out!" He said we can stay here at his house but we have to go get my baby so he can stay too. You have to watch him while we go to Vegas or whatever we do." Looking relieved she says, "That's fine by me, I'll get up and get dressed and go get the baby now." Diamond sounded annoyed and said, "Good hurry up and get out so I can start cleaning this house."

37
CHAPTER
❖
THE UNWANTED GUEST

It was stuff everywhere, make-up was all in the bathroom, the rugs in the bathroom were soaked from her mom taking a shower. Her mother left without folding her covers and left them on the couch. Her clothes were scattered on the floor because she was looking for something to wear to her sister's house to go get the baby. Diamond finished cooking breakfast and started cleaning up, while I kicked back on the couch puffing a blunt and watching T.V. I took this opportunity to call my Big Bruh to tell him the good news about me knocking another hoe. He answers the phone with a huge smile that you could hear, "What's up lil brah how's the pimpin going?" I respond with a smile from ear to ear and say, "It's going cool big brah, but I want your advice on something. I sit up on the couch at attention and explain, "Alright, I knocked this bitch at the Strip club a few weeks ago, and the bitch is ready to fuck with me and go to Vegas, but the bitch got a bad ass mouth on her. She got a momma that ain't got no place to stay and lives out of her car. Plus, the bitch got a baby. Now, do you think this bitch is worth me pimping on her?" Big Bruh says, "Well, you got to be versatile with style in order to be a pimp lil brah, you got to be a man first. You are going to have to make sacrifices for certain hoes if you want your game to be right." He continued, "Then to each his own little brother, for you I would say go ahead and test the waters, but for a pimp like me, I ain't got time to be dealing with no hoe and her dysfunctional ass family. You can't lose faith in the game you have to believe in it. Do you think the bitch can make you millions?" At attention and on que I respond, "Yeah I think so." Big Bruh exhaled and said, "Then follow your heart and pimp on her ass real good." When you get to Vegas make sure you network till your neck hurts to get the money, and until the doors fall off, you need to make your journey with the pimpin, a success. It ain't gone be easy I can tell you that, but you have to stay down with it in order to get something out of it. What happened to the bitch you took down to Vegas the first time?" Looking like I just got called for my fifth foul in a basketball game I said, "That episode had a Ying and a Yang twist to it big brah, the bitch made me more money than I invested in her. But she ended up at some other hoes house. The other hoes pimp, put a mickey in the bitch's drink and now the bitch is half retarded." Big Bruh asked, "Dam lil brah is that right? It sounds like it was a lack of pimpin on your part." Sheepishly I responded, "Yeah I know I felt hella bad about it, but I got over it." Big Bruh was light weight scolding me and said, "Well this time stay on top of your game and don't get sidetracked. I wanted to tell you that you shouldn't have taken that bitch down to Vegas yet without at least trying her on the track out here. You gotta understand she was a **turn out** and never ever did no hoeing yet. You just took the bitch out the fish tank and threw her in the ocean with the sharks, but I had to let you learn from your mistakes and get your experience on. You would've done it anyway without listening, all you wanted to do was go to Vegas and pimp." Confirming what he was saying I said, "Yeah you right big brah, I probably wouldn't have listened and done it anyway, let me get back to this pimpin and I'll hit you up later." Big Bruh said, "Alright lil-bro I'll talk to you in a minute" and we both hung up. Turning my attention to Diamond I said, "A bitch, have you ever done any freelance hoeing while you worked at that Strip club?" Seeming unphased she answers, "No daddy this will be my first time walking the track to make some money. While folding clothes she says, "At the Strip club we ain't got to worry about finding the tricks because they come to us." I said, "Well bitch I'm not going to just through you out in Vegas like that without at least trying you out on the track in Frisco. You got to be sharp, the last bitch I brought out to Vegas ended up getting a mickey laced in her drink by some other hoe and her pimp and it kind of made the bitch slow. I don't won't no more bad shit on my conscience so I will see how you handle the Frisco track. I'll be certain that you will be able to make it." Looking perplexed she asked, "How did she end up in the presence of another pimp and another hoe? I know she didn't think she had a hoe friend, did she? Hoes always try to knock another hoe and bring them to their pimp, that's one of the oldest tricks in the book." I hesitantly said, "Uh naw bitch it's a long story" not wanting to let her know that that's what really happened. "We will go to Frisco when your momma comes back with your son" She nodded her head yes and said, "OK daddy, I'm almost finished cleaning so I'll be ready when she gets here." Her mother finally arrived with the baby and brought him into the house. He was a cute little dude light skinned, brown eyes about two or three years old. Diamond picked up her son giving him a big hug and a kiss. He started kicking and wiggling his feet for her to put him down and said, "Well forget you then Blaxton, you don't want momma to hug you?" Her son said, "Leave me alone momma you bitch!" I started smiling trying hard not to laugh because for one, it was cute, but then again, I knew it wasn't cool. Christy said, "Blaxton don't talk like that to your mother she misses you." He blurted back quickly before his grandmother could finish her sentence and said, "Fuck you grandma!" *This little scene was something out of comic book* I thought. Here I am in my apartment with this hoe that I knocked, her mother and her son, who don't have no respect for each other. I didn't want to take the chance to get cussed out by a two-year-old baby but did it anyway." I reluctantly said, "What's up lil homie?" As I positioned my hand to give the little baby a high five. He quipped, "What's up?" and gave me a high five. They were shocked because Blaxton didn't even know who I was, but he gave me a high five and was being cool with me. I asked the baby, "Are you thirsty?" and he replied by shaking his head yes. So, I dug into his baby bag and got his bottle out and said, "You want milk or juice?" Blaxton excitedly said, "Juice!" I gave the kid his bottle and asked him if I could pick him up and hold him. He reached up for me to pick him up, then he settled into my arms with his bottle in his mouth. After I held the baby for about five minutes saying what's up and asking him his name, I felt my arm getting hot and wet from holding him. Calmly I said, "Diamond won't you change his diaper, its sagging and leaking piss all over the place." She grabbed her baby and he started yelling and kicking for her to let him go. Then she yelled saying "Shut yo ass up before I beat yo ass! You need yo dam diaper changed, don't nobody want to be holding no pissy ass baby." He still screamed and acted a fool all the way until she finished changing his diaper and when she finished, he stood up and said, "Momma you bitch." They laughed thinking it was cute and I thought to myself, *dam I guess this is how this family gets down*. Fuck it, I joined in with them and laughed too.

38
CHAPTER
❖
DOWN AND OUT BAD

Diamond and I made it to the track in San Francisco. Ole girl was ready to strut her stuff so she could show me that she knew what she was doing. She already had a cellphone, so I ran the game down to her before she got out my SUV. Diamond got out of my truck and started walking doing her thing without waving and blowing kisses like J.J. used too. I gamed her ass up for starters but wanted to see what type of bitch she was for real. I decided to call my pimp patna to get on Diamond to see if she would stay firm or fall like a domino. I hopped out my truck and dialed up the pimps' number and got his voice mail saying, "You've reached me playa, your Highness the bay area's finest, if you want to live stress free leave a message for me "Beep!" I left him a message telling him that I was on the track in Frisco and wanted him to return my call. I hung up and started walking to the pool hall to play some eight ball. I waited for Diamond or the pimp to hit me back, which ever one hit me first. As I was passing by a bunch of homeless people laying in their cardboard boxes and begging for change. I took out a fist full of five-dollar bills so that I could give it to the homeless people. That was my way to give back to the community, don't judge me niggas. I passed out a few five-dollar bills and noticed one of the homeless families I was walking towards. I asked, "Grandma is that you?" An older lady looked up at me and answered in a lowly tone, "Hey baby how are you doing?" Now this is not my maternal grandmother, but it was my little homie Dave-baby grandmother! "I'm good, so this is where y'all migrated too huh?" Grandmother inhaled and then exhaled and said, "Yeah this is where we are… unfortunately." Of course, I'm still concerned about all of them because I used to kick it with them hella hard. Especially after all of those good home cooked meals and fried fish and shit. Being inquisitive I asked, "Where is El-bogey and Ivory?" Sadly, grandmother looked up at me and said, "Oh baby you ain't heard? El-bogey died about 3 weeks ago, she overdosed and died on crack. She just couldn't take the fact that someone had taken her son Dave-baby's life behind the back of that dead end street." Those feelings that I had suppressed began to come up and I felt a sharp pain in my stomach like someone was pulling my insides out. I kept my shit together and said, "Dam grandma, I'm sorry to hear that and I'm sorry somebody took Dave-baby out like that too." I said, "Well where is Ivory?" Stoically she responded, "Ivory done got caught stealing in one of these stores out here for the fifth time. Them people done put her ass in jail and I told her to stop stealing because these people out here don't play that shit. I told her that they will put yo ass in a cage and forget about you, but she didn't listen. I no she is some were sitting in somebody's jail doing time." She shook her head in a disgraceful manner looking on the ground about to kneel and pick up the butt of a cigarette off the ground. I stopped her before she did and hugged her with all my might. Rocking back and forth with her I told her that everything was going to be alright and for her to stay strong. I gave her the remaining fistful of five-dollar bills that were in my hand. With a quivering voice I asked, "Is this where I can find you?" Grandma with tears coming down the side of her face said, "Don't feel sorry for us "bay-bee" we put this on ourselves. Nobody made us smoke crack and become a drug infested family. We made that decision on our own. Just make sure you don't end up dead, or in jail, or a dope fiend like us. Let our life experience be a life lesson to you, understand?" Finally, the tears started to break through, and I couldn't hold them back any longer and I told grandma I wouldn't become a victim of crack. Apologizing for what had happened to all of her family and that I loved her. She mustered up a smile and patted me on my shoulder, letting me know that she was a survivor and that she would be alright. We both knew that that was a lie. The whole family was down and out real bad. We hugged one more time and I assured her that I would be back in a couple of weeks to check in on her before I moved to Las Vegas. I had to shake that shit off and I continued to walk to the pool hall to shoot some eight ball.

I received a call from my pimp patna, and he said, "Hey young pimpin, what's happen with you?" I replied, "Nothing much big pimp I'm just out here testing the waters to see if this new bitch I knocked is a bread winner before I relocated down to Las Vegas." The pimp said, "Are you alright it sounds like your heart is in the game, but your spirits need to be reenergized?" literally dusting myself off as I talk to him, I said, "I'm cool pimpin, I just ran into some old folks from the neighborhood who I used to look out for, they are out here homeless and doing bad." Understanding why I'm feeling like this he responds, "That's all part of the game young pimpin, you just make sure you stay on top of your game, so you don't fall short and get the shit end of the stick like they did." Seems like everybody is telling me to stay on top of my game or stay out of jail or stay off the drugs. Pushing forward I asked, "Are you coming out on the blade any time soon?" Sensing that I was ready to move on from me and my problems he says, "Yeah of course, I'll be out there in about half an hour or so. My bitches are already out there, and I need to come and check my trap if you know what I mean." I agreed and said, "I know what you mean pimping well, when you get here hit me up because I want to see if this bitch is one hundred or not. I need you to get at her and send a few of your hoes after her to see if she gone bar-b-que or mildew." Accepting the challenge the pimp says, "It's all good young pimpin give me a few and I'll meet you at the pool hall so we can rap a taste about it." I was happy and said, "Aite cool I preciate ya" and hung up the phone. I went through the front door of the pool hall, as usual everybody stopped what they were doing and paused with their conversations. When they realized it wasn't the police, they went back to their business routine. I acknowledged them back with a head nod and started my game of eight ball. After waiting for about thirty minutes, the pimp came in, He was wearing a three-piece suit that was all yellow with a yellow silk shirt, and a vest, with yellow gator shoes. His hair is long and silky down past his shoulders and he had two of his hoes walking behind him with their heads down. The people at the pool hall cheered and roared as he made his grand entrance slapping fives and touching hands with other pimps, players, hustlers, and hoes. He saw me at the table shooting pool and strolled his way over to me with his gators clacking against the floor with his two red light wives behind him. He walks up to me maintaining eye contact all the way and snapped his fingers. His two ladies went and retrieved a chair for him to sit it down. One of the hoes that he had with him is at least six one, early thirties, average looking, chocolate, slender build like she used to run track, with a short black hair cut that goes to her ears. She wore a black choker to match her emerald, green dress and fish net stockings. The other hoe that he had with him is five nine, late twenties, cute face, the color of a cardboard box, big sad eyes, thick like a bowl of biscuits and gravy. She wore a burgundy and black dress with blonde hair slightly covering her face. He snapped again and waved his arm away from him so that they can mind their business. The pimp sat down, crossed his legs, smiled at me and said, "Young pimpin how's life treating ya?" I'm thinking *like what's up with the rhetorical questions?* Hell, you know that I ain't got it like you do right about now. Anyways, I responded, "Its treating me accordingly, but if I had your hand, I would cut mines off!" While laughing the pimp said, "Stay down young pimpin stay down, so what's up with this new bitch you said you got? I was giving him some info about her profile and said, "She's pretty cool, the bitch came with a lot of luggage but it's part of the game. I'm on my way to make a move to Las Vegas and I want to test the bitch out before I take that route. The last bitch that I took down there was kind of green to the game and ended up having some bad luck. All I need for you to do is try and knock the bitch from me and if you do, this will be the second hoe you knocked from me and you can have her." Rubbing his hands like to keep them warm he responded, "You got it young pimpin you know I would never pass up a chance to knock another bitch" he said with all sixty-two teeth showing." I asked him, "Whatever happened to that one bitch named Sasha you knocked from me?" Wiping the air like he doesn't want anymore he said, "That bitch ended up going down like super head. The bitch was hardheaded and didn't want to listen to my instructions and ended up getting snatched up by the San Francisco city vise police. I would've called "our boy" to bail the bitch out, but when a hoe doesn't listen to my instructions and get caught up in self distraction, I wash my hands of the bitch. Then he snapped his fingers once more, and his two women came and stood behind him with the heads down. He gave his bitches specific instructions and said, "You bitches go out there and do your best to knock me my patnas hoe. She should be the newest bitch out on the track hoeing." He continued, "If y'all do, I'll give you this Anaconda, sugar dick, that I got between my legs." Then he said, "Now get!" and his two bitches ran out of the pool like the fire alarm was ringing. Turning to me the pimp said, "That ought to get them bitches motivated because I know dam well, I hardly ever give them some of this sweet royale meat." I cracked a smile and thanked my pimp patna and asked, if he would do me the honors of playing me in a few rounds of 8 ball.

39
CHAPTER
❖
THE TEST RUN

Meanwhile, on the track, the pimps two hoes spotted Diamond getting out of a car after serving a customer. They approached her and said, "Hey girl how's the track treating a bitch this evening?" She knew that cordial conversation was allowed amongst hoes because all of them tried to stick together when it came to the vice or danger when were out here hustling. So, she replied "It's been cool so far, I haven't seen any undercovers or came across no crazy ass tricks since I been out here." She started heading the opposite direction to get away from the pimps two hoes. She was focused and she wanted to keep herself in the spirit of getting money and not in the spirit of congregating. Not giving up easily the pimps girls said, "I never seen you out here before what's your name?" His two ladies were following Diamond as she walked away expeditiously. "My name is Nicole" she lied. "Well Nicole girl we got a daddy that's balling out the game, and he hella fine too." They continued to partition, "He treats us with the upmost respect and gives us plenty of security and stability. He would love for a pretty young thang like you to be on his team. Plus, you seem like you got some class and style, and we wouldn't mind being wife in laws with you. We could do things together and teach and learn things from one another. What do you say you come home with us and give my daddy a chance to turn you into a star?" I could see that she was having just about enough. Diamond stopped and turned toward them recognizing game that these two hoes was trying to knock her and said, "First of all out of respect I thank y'all two for trying to look out for a bitch, but I got a daddy and he got money, security and stability as well. If I was some dumb fickle minded bitch with low self-esteem, scared, and new to the game I might've taken you up on your offer. She was getting a little bit louder because she was appalled that someone would try her and said, "**But**

I'm not, I'm cool and content with the pimp I have right now because I can see he's going places." What y'all need to do is reconsider the pimp y'all dealing with and come home with mines. I don't know what number position y'all are, but I'm my pimps only hoe and if you get on his team now, you can establish some time and earn you some rank and status." With that said Diamond continued to walk away leaving the pimps two bitches looking dumb founded and curious. The two ladies of the pimp went back to the pool hall and told their daddy that she was a stand-up bitch and that they couldn't bring her home. The pimp said, "See that's what I get for sending a hoe to do a pimp's job. Did y'all even catch the bitch's name?" Looking slightly defeated they said, "She said her name was Nicole daddy." Then I interrupted and said, "That ain't the bitch's name. And the pimp with disbelief in his voice said, "See you hoes ain't even get a dam name where is this bitch at, I bet you I knock the hoe. His women told him where they last saw Diamond walking and the pimp headed out the door. The pimp left the pool hall, and his two women was staring at me from a distance in admiration and trying to size me up. They were wondering what it would be like to be my woman instead of the pimp's. They weren't even considered in his stable yet, they were still prospecting. Since Diamond had put something on their minds and told them about how they could accumulate rank and position, I really had their attention without even noticing it. And from the way that I was shooting 8-ball, I acted as if I could care less. The pimp waited outside the pool hall about 2 minutes and stuck his head back through the door and caught his two bitches' reckless eye balling his young pimp patna. I laughed to myself and already knew that I would be giving him a courtesy call about one of the hoes or both of them. So, I made it a mental note to keep them as prospect bitches and pimp on them in the worse way. The pimp headed to where Diamond was last seen walking the track. He finally saw her and walked up to her. When Diamond saw him, she instantly knew he was an experienced pimp by his style and fashion of clothes, so she instantly started walking away. Walking fast towards her he says loudly, "You ain't got to walk away from the pimpin baby run to it, cause if you knew better, you'd do better, fuckin wit some pimpin like this. Ain't no hoe fixing to be hoeing out on my track and she ain't paying me or I don't know the bitch's daddy. You better size up and wise up and choose bitch before I get gangsta on yo hoe ass." Using his extortion approach on Diamond to see if he could scare her into fuckin with him. She kept walking away faster and faster and lost one of her heels then pulled out her cellphone to call me. "Daddy, daddy this pimp is chasing me, and he is scaring the shit out of me!" Already knowing who it was, I played the role and said, "Stop walking from his ass right now and put his ass on the phone!" Daddy I'm scared!" Getting louder I said, "No put his ass on the phone right fuckin now!" Her fight, flight, or freeze responses kicked in and she was frozen. She got enough courage to stop and say, "My pimp has something to say to you for sweating me and holding up his money" as she passed the pimp the phone. The pimp got on the phone and said, "Young playa your bitch is track tested and pimped approved" and we both started laughing like a muthafucka! Looking relieved she didn't catch on so quickly but wondered how he knew her pimp's name. Then it finally hit her, and she got back on the phone and said, "Daddy y'all know each other?" I was trying to stop laughing and said, "Yeah bitch we know each other." Looking dejected she asked, "Did you know them two other bitches that tried to get me on their team?" I responded laughing in her ear, "Yeah bitch that was my pimp patnas two hoes." From the sound of her voice, you could tell tears were starting to well up in her eyes. She asks, "Why you do that daddy" sincerely. I took off and flashed on her and got loud and said, "First of all bitch, don't ask me no muthafuckin questions, second of all bitch, I had to make sure you were ready for the big leagues third of all bitch, I can't keep having a bunch of flaws on my conscious because I can pimp better with a clear mind!" Having a bit more clarity she says, "I'm sorry daddy for asking, I guess I passed the test huh?" I responded snapping, "Yeah bitch you passed, keep getting my money and we will head to get something to eat later on, and put that pimp back on the phone." Acquiescing she gave the phone to the pimp, and I thanked him again and asked him if he was coming back to play some pool. The pimp said that he had some business to tend too and to send his bitches too him, and that he would catch me on the rebound. I then hung up the phone and told his two ladies to go on the track to meet their daddy. As they walked out the door, they both looked back at me like "what's up with it?" and walked out. After a few more hours of playing 8-ball, I called Diamond and told her to meet me back at the truck. When I arrived at the truck, she was already there waiting and happy to see me. She was glad that she passed the test to be my bitch and head off to Las Vegas with me.

40
CHAPTER
❖
WHAT UP VEGAS GUESS WHOSE BACK?

After getting packed up and leaving Diamond's mom Christy at my apartment with Blaxton, we were ready to hit the road. I told myself that I would forbid anything happening to Diamond, while she was fuckin with me like it did with Nina. Driving my truck up to Vegas was like one huge pep talk. She was with it though and understood the game plan. We got to the Strip, and I ran the game down to her again on how our program was going to be handled. She walked ahead and I stayed a few yards behind her as she strutted her stuff and talked to me on the cellphone. As we worked our game down the Strip, I noticed there wasn't a lot of tricks outside. I did however, peep that it was more pimps out sweating hoes and trying to knock one to have. Diamond was clicking her heels trying not to get caught up by any of those cats and was steady maneuvering around them concentrating on her hoeing. She finally caught her a trick and told me where she was going and that she would call when she was finished. I took the liberty to grab a Vegas newspaper to see what type of trucking jobs were available and how much the rent was down here. Searching in the construction section I noticed they had two pages of owner operator positions from various casinos all throughout Vegas. I felt like that was a super plus for me to move down here now, instead of staying in California. Turning to the apartment section, I noticed how cheap the living expenses were and made up my mind that this was definitely where I wanted and needed to be.

Taking out a pen, I marked down a few places that I would call tomorrow after Diamond, and I had breakfast. By the time I finished looking at the newspaper she was finished with her first trick, and I was five hundred dollars richer, and only thirty minutes had passed. She was told to meet me at the casino parking lot to collect the money and get back out there on the stroll. Not long before she got out there, she was calling to let me know that she had another trick before I could even get behind her for support. I told her to handle her business and to call if she gets into any trouble when she got finished. Always keeping my options open, I decided to join the rest of the pimps on the track and started sweating hoes my dam self. There were plenty of pimps riding around circling the blocks and walking, chasing hoes up and down the track. Game recognize game and I noticed these two pimps in particular seemed like the same age that I was. They were on every bitch moving. We caught eye contact with each other but neither of us spoke. Always being cautious I made a mental note of the two pimps and kept it moving. Checking out other possibilities to knock me some more women, I decided to go into one of the casinos to sweat a few carpet hoes. These hoes were running around selling pussy in the casino like it was legal. I thought it must be cool and wanted Diamond to come inside so she could get some money like these carpet bitches. Contemplating that move, I decided to save that for when we moved out here. Looking around, I noticed a few bitches go to the elevator with some other O.G. pimp that was wearing all red. I knew that the bitches going in the elevator with him weren't his by the way he was sweating them and how they were trying to get away from him. That was a good tactic and I wanted to be in the elevator too with the hoes. That way they couldn't leave, and they would have to stand there and listen to what I had to say. I trotted over to where they were and entered the elevator with them. I said, "You bitches may be on the right track but you on the wrong train. I'm a new player on the scene, the best who's doing it that ain't gone ruin it, so let your next move be your best move and fuck wit a pimp that's smooth, with a lot to gain and nothing to lose." The hoes started giggling without giving any eye contact. I spit out my phone number as the bitches came to the floor they were getting off at. They were about to push the button to go back down to the lobby when another bitch came staggering onto the elevator. The bitch was way out of pocket giving plenty eye contact and standing next to me and the O.G. pimp in the all red. As the elevator started to move that's when the O.G. pimp in all red hit the stop button on the elevator and said, "You dirty funky no-good hoe!" In a loud and sinister voice. "You got the nerve to get your drunk **outta pocket** ass on the elevator with two pimps and start reckless eye balling?" Facing and pointing and her in a confrontational way he continues, "**Break yourself right now** before I put yo ass under pimp arrest and tell yo daddy what his bitch is out here doing!" The bitch was so terrified of the way the O.G. pimp had belittled her; she went in her purse and gave him all of the money she had on her. The O.G. pimp snatched the money from her and kept grilling the bitch until we got to the lobby. When the elevator doors opened the bitch sobered up and walked away with her head down through the casino hallway. I looked at him and said, "Dam O.G. that was some serious hardcore guerilla pimpin. I ain't never seen no shit like that. I gots to give you a pimp stripe for that one." Then he said, "That's what I do pimpin I walk around the track outside and in these casinos wearing this all-red outfit catching hoes out and break they ass like I just did this bitch right here. I don't have no hoes right now, so this is how I get my bread and butter. You'd be surprised on how much money I make every night doing that shit." As another hoe walked into his sight he said, "like this silly naive ass bitch right here I just made seven hundred dollars off of this hoe because she was scared shitless of me." Seeing how there are different levels to pimping I said, "I can respect that, I can respect that, I may have to try that mojo a few times and see if it gets me paid." The O.G. said, "You have to catch the scariest vulnerable bitches in order for it to truly work. If you come across a hard head gangsta hoe she just might pull out a knife on you and try to stab you. It don't work on everybody just certain bitches." Appreciating the heads up I say, "I'll keep that in mind O.G. and stepped away from him and called Diamond, "Hello daddy" breathing hella hard barley catching her breath. I respond, "Dam bitch sounds like somebody is working yo ass overtime." She chuckled with embarrassment and said, Yeah, he making sure he gets his money's worth out my ass. It's been an hour and a half so far so that's fifteen hundred. I'm going to try to keep him from coming as long as I can so I can walk up out of here with at least twenty-five hundred." Encouraging her I said, "That's my bitch!" Almost forgetting I said, "A if you ever see a O.G. pimp wearing all red I want you to run like hell and stay 50 feet away from him." Alright daddy let me get back to this trick before he gets suspicious O.K. I'll call you when I'm done" then she hung up the phone. So, I continued to stay in hot pursuit of a new prostitute the whole night until Diamond and I were finally tired. We talked with each other over breakfast about one another's night, then headed for the hotel to get some sleep.

41
CHAPTER
❖
THE HEIST

We woke up the next day it wasn't quite primetime yet, so I decided to take a tour of Vegas. We got into the Expedition and rode around Vegas admiring the attractions. We did some shopping and a little bit of gambling and got our bellies full and headed back to the room to get ready for the night to come. She was really feeling herself from the money she had made the night before and was looking extra sexy. Not to be out done, I was feeling pretty sexy my dam self. I had me some extra classic threads to look like a millionaire. We set out for the night and did our same routine. It wasn't long before she got a nibble and was off to a tricks hotel to have a little fun. I did my usual "thang" chasing hoes and sweating them. Out here in these streets I happen to see those same two pimps that kept looking at me the other day. Still not speaking but we made eye contact and did the universal "head nod" to acknowledge one another and kept it pushing. Diamond called me saying that this trick that she was fooling with has about ten or fifteen thousand dollars on him. Sounding irritated she says, "This muthafucka only wants to spend thirty minutes with me so that's only five hundred dollars for you. I was trying my best to get him to spend some more or to catch him slipping and run out the hotel, but he ain't giving in. Come rob this muthafucka so we can get him for all he's got!" At the end of the day, it's all about the money and I'm down for getting it by any means. I responded, "Yeah bitch that's a good idea I see you got yo hoe antennas tuned in to the right channel tonight huh? I'll be there in about fifteen minutes when I knock one-time bitch, you'll no that's me, then open the door." Snickering dastardly she says, "Alright daddy." Getting into my truck I left the track in a hurry to go rob the trick for that money. As I walked closer to the hotel where Diamond was at with the trick. I thought to myself, *dam what the fuck am I going to rob his ass with?* Then I said fuck it! I'll just strong arm his ass, but then I figured that was too violent and this game ain't supposed to inflict no kind of violence. My fucking stomach started turning into knots and I felt a little uneasy about robbing the trick. So, I called my consultant/oldest brother to see if he could give me some game about what he would do in a situation like this. "What's up big brah?" He responded loudly, "Ain't nothing up but the same channel just on a different program lil brah, what up with you?" Without hesitation I went on in and said, "Big brah the bitch got a trick at the hotel holding out on spending some real dough with her and he is flashing it around. He has about ten or fifteen thousand dollars in front of the bitch but only wants to spend five hundred dollars for thirty minutes with her." With a quick response Big Bruh said, "And what, let me guess you want to rob him for his money don't you?" I spoke up and said "Exactly" while laughing. It felt like he was heated when he told me, "Lil-brah, you got to learn to be fair with the game if you want the game to be fair with you. I don't think you should rob the trick just because he doesn't want to spend all of his money with your bitch. You could catch a charge fuckin around with this bitch. He annoyedly continued and said, "You definitely don't want to catch a robbery charge in a city and state that you ain't from, especially in Vegas. It would cost you way more than ten or fifteen thousand dollars on lawyer fees alone. And you know if they catch the bitch and not you, she gone sing like Kelly Price. So, what you do is play like the bitch is your wife and you are busting the bitch with some dude to make him feel guilty then you mention that you know he paid for sex so that would make him feel even more guilty and he would know he broke the law. Angrily you keep ranting and raving going through his pockets and stuff, telling him if he pays you some money you won't go to the cops. And watch him start giving you everything he's got. That way he can't say you robbed him if it goes all bad, the only thing, he can say is he met some guy's woman and offered her money in exchange for sex and he ain't gone want to say that to incriminate his self trust me." My mind was fucking blown! My brother could've been a writer or something because that was some good shit that he came up with on the fly. I delightfully responded, "Man big brah if it wasn't for you, I would've been fell on my face with this pimpin. You're the reason why I can stay above it and once again thanks for some more of it." Alright with a change of plans, I'm about to drop a line on this bitch and give her a heads up on my plan and I'll get back at you." We hung up from each other and I called Diamond to let her know how to play along with my plan. I mapped out the plan and went to the location were the trick and her were staying at. I knocked one time on the door giving her my que. She opened the door with nothing on to make it seem like they were caught in the act and said, "Oh shit my husband is at the door!" That was my que to act a fool and I delivered. I said boomingly, "Bitch what the fuck are you doing in this hotel walking around naked!?" I barged my way through the hotel door and slammed it. "Who the fuck is this muthafucka laying in the bed, I know y'all didn't just get finished fuckin, I know y'all didn't just get finished fuckin." I said it in a roar with tension and insecurity in my voice and a frown that wanted to kill with my eyes all big and shit. Returning my energy for the best Oscar she said, "No baby it's not what you think. I got lost trying to find the hotel to take a shower and this gentleman was nice enough to let me use his." trying to sound convincing. I pretended fuming and say, "I saw yo ass outside a few hours ago talking to this muthafucka and followed you up here! It show didn't look like you were lost as fast as you came up to his hotel room." By that time the trick sat up on the bed and said with fear and nervousness, "No sir we weren't having sex I just wanted to help the young lady out." The trick is a middle age white dude, curly pepper hair, body looked like a fucking thanksgiving turkey uncooked, and his height was about five eight. I cut him off in a boisterous tone and continued to say, "Do I look stupid to you, it smells like booty, dick and pussy in this muthafucka and you telling me y'all didn't have sex, Man I'm gone kill yo ass up in here and when the police get here, I'm gone tell them that you were having sex with my wife, and I did it out of the heat of passion!" I half speed charged toward him with hands out like I was going to choke him to death. His fight, flight, or freeze kicked in and he was petrified and atrophied to the bed headboard. "Wait Sir please don't kill me I'm sorry. She said she was a prostitute and wanted to make a few hundred dollars by having a little fun." He scurried to the other side of the room, trying to stay away from me with the covers on him not wanting to show his nakedness." I flashed on him like I was extremely offended and say, "You saying my wife is a prostitute now?" I'm really going to choke the shit out of yo ass!" Running behind him faking to attempt to catch him, he is terrified and shrieks, "Look Mister I'm sorry. I'm sorry please don't hurt me. I'm a successful businessman with a good reputation plus I have 3 kids and a wife, please don't kill me or hurt me. I'll give you anything you want to let this misunderstanding cease!" Me sensing that I'm getting close to getting what I wanted says, "I don't want nothing you got but your life" with fire in my eyes. Like an epiphany he consents to me and says, "I have over ten thousand dollars in the pocket of my black slacks near the bar suite please, you can take that. We can forget that this thing ever happened." I stopped in mid stride and repeated what he said, "You got over ten thousand dollars in your slacks?" with a look of shock on my facial expression. "Bitch go look in his pants pocket and see if this muthafucka is lying so I don't beat his ass." Diamond was already dressed and walked to where his slacks were and checked for the money. A fist full of hundreds fell to the floor as she kneeled down to pick up the money. Then I said, "Well, I guess we can act as if this never happened, you need to stop buying pussy because you can endanger yourself or end up in jail." I said it like I really cared whether or not the trick would end up in jail. "Come on baby let's get out of this nasty ass hotel and go home we ain't never coming back to

Vegas!" Exiting the hotel and back on the Strip, we laughed at the whole thing all the way back to our hotel. I really didn't want to leave Vegas, but we had to, because Diamond's son and her mother were still back at the crib. As we left Vegas and drove back to Cali, I hoped that what we did to the trick never comes back on me…I hoped.

42

CHAPTER

❖

SAY IT AIN'T SO

A week later I confirmed with my mother that I was making a move to Vegas for good. She just wished me the best, and that was that. I wanted to make one last stop in Frisco to holla at my pimp patna and to check on Dave-baby's grandmother and give them the news. I made a phone call to my pimp patna to see if he could meet me at the pool hall so that we can chop it up. He told me that he would be on his way to meet me there in thirty minutes. Meanwhile I went to go check on Dave-baby's grandmother to make sure she was okay. I wanted to give her a couple of hundred dollars when I see her again. She was in the same spot panhandling as the rest of the homeless people. She saw me and asked, "Hey bay-bee what's going on I see you came back to check on an old bitch." I chuckled because I knew that she was drunk. She continued on to say, "These muthafucka's out here don't want to give a bitch no change today. But that's alright I still got over half of that money you gave me a week ago." She pulled out the money that I had given her before I left for my trip to Vegas. She then put it back in her pocket so nobody could see it and said, "I probably got moe money than all these homeless muthafucka's out there." Feeling bad for her I said, "Well I came to give you a few more hundred to add to your stash." Facetiously she says, "Good that will help me buy some dishes and something to sit on when I get put in an old folks' home." She stated that, "The county has accepted to pay for her living arrangements as long as she lives." I'm glad to hear that and I gave her a couple hundred dollars. I told her I don't know the next time that I would see her again because I was moving to Las Vegas. She smiled warmly and wished me good luck. She hugged me tight and said, "I guess this means our season in each other's life is up." She also said quickly, "Be careful out there fuckin around in Las Vegas, I heard they don't play that shit out there."

Reassuring her that the message was received I said, "I will grandma, I will." She pulled on my shoulder and said, "O yeah guess whose smoking crack now?" *I hated playing charades,* but I tried to think for a minute and said, "I don't know grandma you got me who?" While shaking her head with a smile as if this shit was funny and said, "That muthafucka Dee!" I gasped and put my closed fist to my mouth because I couldn't believe it, say it ain't so! She continued and said, I seen his ass out here with some old crackhead ass hoe trying to get some money turning tricks. Then he came and bought some crack from one of the dealers out here that be hustling. I was standing right next to him, and he didn't even notice me! That muthafucka done went from sugar to shit, In no time." Already knowing the scenario, J.J. my first hoe, got Dee hooked on that shit. He should've known better when J.J. was sucking his dick dry. I'm not gone lie, this one kind of hurt me. It hurt me to see a young potential playa go out like that, but I figured that's life. This shit made him keep tricking with her every chance he got, and he didn't think that that would happen to him because he knew the type of bitch that she was. If you are a weak individual, then you don't have no business near this shit. This situation made me think about how my other brother got turned out by a bitch dam, hope all goes well for Dee. Starting to leave I gave grandma one last hug and continued to go meet my patna the pimp at the pool hall so I could holla at him before I moved to Vegas. finally, I made it to the pool hall and walked through the door, it was the same routine. The people stopped then continued their business. I did the "universal head nod" to the other players and they obliged. My pimp patna came walking through the door about twenty minutes after I did. His appearance was off to me, I felt that something was wrong because the pimp…didn't look nothing like himself. This time he wasn't being flamboyant he didn't seem like the pimp that I had been seeing for the past few months. He was wearing some sweatpants, a pair of run-down Nikes and a cheap white -T-shirt. He acknowledged me and told me to re-rack the game so that we could start all over. While racking the pool table balls, I said, "I won't be seeing you for a while." Looking confused he looked up at me trying to figure out what I was saying that for. He blurted out, "Vegas was that good to you huh?" Shaking my head yes and with a slit of a smile I answered, "Yeah it was," He forced a fake laugh and asked, "Got all your shit together?" As we are moving around the table I said, "Yep" Not too congratulatory he said, "I hope you know your jumping out the pot and into the frying pan!" Speaking up for myself I said, "I'm just broadening my horizons, plus I want to get some of that Vegas money." Still not being happy for me he said, "Everything that glitters ain't gold young pimpin, and if your mojo ain't broke, ain't no since in fixing it." But I understand how you feel and what you feel you must do. You got my honor on your decision once you get settled down. The pimp asked, "Has that one bitch you bailed out of jail been going to her court dates?" I told him, that bitch was a one hit wonder, and that bitch done started smoking crack. He told me that he was sorry for my loss and that she was a good hoe. Reminiscing I looked at him and grinned remembering how one of his bitches was out of pocket. The pimp looked back at me and nodded his head remembering how he faked like he walked out of the pool hall and doubled back and caught the hoe looking at me with googly eyes but kept it playa playa. Don't trip though young pimpin it happens to the best of us, it's part of the game." My curiosity was peaked, and I said, "Why did you ask me about that bitch?" He quickly responded, "I've been seeing our friend the bail bondsmen coming through the track and he has been circling like he's looking for somebody or something." The pimp with a matter-of-fact attitude says, "If that bitch ain't been going to her court dates, that means he had to pay that whole bond. He's either looking to pick the bitch up and bring her to jail or he's looking to collect his collateral you used to get the bitch out." Then it dawned on me! "Dam I put my Expedition up for collateral for that bitch to get out." The pimp looked up at me and said, "Young pimpin you better hope that muthafucka is not out riding around circling the block and found your truck." Shit! I said, "let me get my ass up out of here before I fuck around and don't have no car when I go to Las Vegas!" I stopped in the middle of the pool game and gave the pimp some dap and a hug and told him that I would holla at him when I got settled in. Rushing to where my car was parked to see if it was still safe, I find out that it was not there. It was gone. The only thing that I looked at was an empty parking space. I hesitated for a few minutes then got my thoughts together, and said, "Dam I done lost my Expedition fuckin around with an irresponsible ass hoe." I called the pimp and asked what should I do about the bail bondsman taking my truck? He told me that, "Mostly everything that happens to a pimp is his own fault because the hoes don't run nothing but their mouths. Pimpin is the brains behind the operation so the only thing you can do is blame it on pimpin." That slogan that he said stuck in my head like gorilla glue. *"Blame it on pimpin"* I said. Then if that's the case I got a lot to blame on pimpin and I ain't even been in the game a whole year yet! The pimp told me to notify the bail bondsman and see what he could do. When I called the bail bondsman, he told me he needed fifteen thousand because that was the bond cost to get J.J. smoked out ass out of jail. I had the money but not to spend on getting my fucking truck back. After all the money J.J. had given me, it was useless. Profiting nothing, the game god came and staked his claim. **Blame it on pimpin** basically means, blame it on yourself and the game you live for. Thinking in my head what my Big Bruh had told me. He said verbatim, "*What you gone do when the game gets rough, are you going to give up and tuck your tail between your ass and go in the corner and pout, or are you going to rise to the occasion?* Blame it on pimpin I said it again. I blame the fact that J.J. started smoking crack on pimpin. I could blame the fact that Kay-Kay stole all my money and dope on pimpin. I can blame the fact that I got knocked for Sasha on pimpin. I can blame the fact that Nina got a *mickey* slipped in her drink on pimpin, and now I could blame the fact that my Expedition got repossessed on pimpin. But did this make me feel depressed and walk with my head down? He'll naw, what makes you a man in this game is, the quicker you fall down the quicker you come back up! "Church!" Swallowing my pride, I stood up straight with my head held high as the sky. Put my hands in my pocket and started walking to the nearest Bart station. I was walking with a stroll out of this world, fuck it without a care in the world! like a straight stomp down 100% pimp. I got on the Bart leaving S.F. and when arrived at the Hayward Bart Station. I called Diamond to pick me up, it was a good thing that I allowed them to stay at my house. I'm going to have to use Christy's car as a taxi until I bought me another one. Diamond came to the Bart and picked me up. She asked, "Daddy what happened to you, why are you on the Bart and not driving your Expedition"? I responded drily, "Fuckin around with a bitch that I had before you who got herself snatched up by San Francisco vice and went to jail. I had to put my truck up as a bond to get the bitch out and the hoe never went to court. The bail bondsmen came and repoed my shit to get their money." With a look of concern on her face she asks, "Does this mean we ain't going to Vegas?" I snapped back pridefully and say, "Hell naw bitch that ain't nothing but a minor setback for a major come back, we at Vegas by all means! I will just have to push a rental car around until I can get me another one. Feeling my optimism she smiles and says, "Well don't worry daddy, I will hoe extra hard to get you out of that rental and into something way better than the Expedition, okay? That just gives you enough time to figure out what kind of car you want to buy." I smiled with the thought of Diamond being down with me whether I was on top or climbing to get there. Shit that says a lot about a woman. Most hoes see a pimp start slipping and be on the first thing smoking to fuck with another pimp.

43
CHAPTER

❖

THE MOVE

We got home and the house was looking dusted and disgusted as usual. But I didn't care, I had other things on my mind. The movers came over and they would load up the U-Haul to get us prepared for Vegas. Before we were about to leave Christy had a shit fit. With her eyes big as hell like her personal boat was taking on water she screeched, "What about me and Blaxton?" I could help you guys out down there. I can let you guys use my car since yours got repossessed. Also, I can babysit while y'all go out on the town to make money." After pondering what she was saying and thought that it was a good idea. Diamond lit her ass up and said, "Bitch don't nobody want yo ass hanging around and whining and fuckin up shit. We can't afford to take care of your old ass. And quit trying to use my baby as an escape goat. He has a place to live at my aunties house. You the one that's always homeless and ain't got no place to live. You already used us to have a place to lay your head and get a few hundred dollars, you need to appreciate that." I intervened into their argument and told her mother that I would send her a couple of hundred dollars a month to help her out until we got established. That hushed her up …for now. I turned my attention to my mental check list to make sure that I took care of all the things that I needed to do before leaving. I remembered that I wanted to put my trucking company business on the internet. So, I called and paid for a web address then called Nina to see if it was still cool for her to put it up for me. Calling Nina was a trip, but I called her anyway to get that handled for me. Plus, I had to check in with her and see how she was doing. She was cordial and replied, "Yeah baby I'm getting better, I just been trying to get myself together and stop snorting cocaine." I've been going to church and pursuing my education and my dream to be a web tech engineer. I haven't been the same since that trip to Las Vegas I took with you but I'm slowly getting back. She continued giving me an update about herself and said, "I would've been calling to keep in contact with you but, I'd probably want some more of that good cocaine you be having for sell. I'm trying to make it back to myself again and there's no telling what I would've done to get it." Nodding my head in agreement I said, "I understand how you feel Nina, maybe that trip was a blessing in disguise because if you wouldn't have gone you wouldn't be trying to get yourself together." They say the Lord works in mysterious ways." Then I continued, "Hey is it still cool if you do my website for me? Without a second thought she said, "Sure baby I can do that for you, and I will still do it for free." I appreciated it but I said, "You don't have do it for free I will pay you at least three or four hundred dollars" laughing she responds, "I don't think I can stand the sight of seeing you right now because I'm too weak. I might want to do something I have no business doing just to be with you like I did last time." She laughed subtly and said, "You are a powerful man, and I don't think you realize how much power you possess over people." Man, I said to myself, *she makes me feel like I'm one of the devils' advocate or something.* Like bad things are just going to start happening if she even sees me. Then who could blame her, because ever since she met me, she wrecked her car, snorted more cocaine than a little bit, started selling her body for money and drugs. And to top it off, she got a mickey put in her drink that made her almost handicapped. Thinking about what she said I digressed and said, "I feel you; I would stay away from me too if I was you." She got all my information for the web address and website and told me to give her at least a week and it would be up. I graciously thanked her, and we ended our conversation.

44

CHAPTER

❖

THE FACTION

Diamond and I finally arrived in Las Vegas; I felt a sense of relief. I finally made it to **the pimp and hoe Side Show** City. The first thing I did was pay for one of those weekly rooms and got a rental car and started calling apartment numbers for applications and interviews. Checking out the area I visited several apartments, but the one that I wanted wasn't going to be ready for at least a month. Unfortunately, Diamond and I would have to stay at the weekly room until then. Expenses are starting to pile up on me because, I must pay fifty dollars a week for the room, plus an extra five hundred dollars a week to keep my furniture in the U-Haul, and another five hundred a week for me to have the rental. Since I no longer sold drugs. Now, I would have to depend on Diamond and the game to make ends meet. Before night fall, I went and did a quick tour around the hotel that we were staying at to find out where the other pimps and hoes lived in the hotel like us. On my way back to the hotel to rest for a while, I saw those other two pimps that I kept bumping into while I was out here pimpin a couple of weeks ago in Las Vegas. Things were moving on the Strip as it does every night, and we were doing our thang. I ran my same routine on Diamond to get the money and for some reason the tricks weren't biting like they did a few weeks ago. This happened for a whole week, and we didn't make not one red cent! One night on our way to the hotel coming in from a long night of pimpin and hoeing. Not making a dime, I was feeling a little depressed and discouraged. I saw those other two pimps that I kept seeing around that was staying at the same hotel we were staying at. They were walking from the Strip to the hotel I assumed, and they started throwing their hands up and waving at me like they were hailing for a cab. I decided to stop and see what the problem was as one of the pimps said, "A what's up pimpin I don't mean to be a burden on you but are

137

you on your way to the hotel, and if you are is it cool if me and my boy get a ride from you?" He continued, "We just came back from the track sweating bitches all night and we tired as fuck." Not feeling threatened I figured it was cool, plus I admired their tenacity a little bit. To walk all the way to the track from the hotel because it was quite a way, that showed me that they were loyal and determined just like I was. "Yeah, it's cool pimpin I'll give y'all a ride" and they hoped in my rental car. They introduced themselves as Smooth and Lil-pimp. I spoke up and said, they call me Big Dawg were y'all from?" Looking at each other to decide which one would go first and in unison they both said, "We from Oakland." Surprised I said, "Y'all from the town?" and looked at them both in my rearview trying to study their faces to see if I recognized them. Proudly I responded, "Me too" and we reminisced about Oakland and its hard times. When we arrived at the hotel, I observed the **dynamic duo** appearances up close. Smooth had the look like he was a straight pimp. He had his hair in a mushroom hairstyle that looked like he permed it too much. But he was ready to strut with his full-length blazer coat, with some loafers, and slacks. Lil-pimp looked kind of like a D-boy with some Nike Air Max's on, jeans and a white t-shirt. Then I said, "Lil-pimp, I seen a movie with an O.G. pimp from Frisco that called himself **The Pimp**. Why did you take somebody else's name?" Lil-pimp looked at me stone faced and said, "I didn't take his name that's my father's name." I was hella shocked and said, "Is that right? Looking surprised I said to him, "Bruh, So you the son of a celebrity pimp?" I started monologuing about how I can't wait till my pimpin get up like his reputation. "Man, he could knock bitch's off of his name alone!" Lil-pimp started smiling because I realized who he was. Smooth interrupted and said, "how's the game treating you down here?" I responded, "It was treating me better when I was just coming through on the weekends, but since I moved down here it's been kind of shaky." Trying to be encouraging Smooth said, "it will get better, you just have to stay down and pimp hard every day. I noticed you and your bitch be out on the track most of the time. You need to give that bitch a few dollars and send her ass through them casinos and have the bitch play some slots or something and plot on tricks in there gambling. I bet you'll start having better days." Appreciating the knowledge I said, "I'm gone take that into consideration, where y'all hoes at?" I stated, "I always see y'all two, but I never see y'all hoes." Lil-pimp answered, "I don't have a hoe right now, I'm in high pursuit of a new prostitute as we speak!" Smooth said, "My hoe got caught up down here on five different hoe cases, so now she chills in the room. We just do our thing off the internet. When the bitch gets a call, she hops in the cab and goes where the trick is and handle her business." I thought to myself, *dam just from talking to this nigga Smooth he already gave me two new ideas to pimp on Diamond.* And just like that we formed a faction. I'm going to make sure I stayed on good terms with him because he seems to know a lot about pimpin out here in Las Vegas. I said, "Well here pimpin, y'all put this number in your cellphones and we'll stay in touch, you know pimpin gots to stick together." Everyone exchanged numbers and went to their rooms. The next day I illuminated Diamond to let her know that we are going to run our game a little different. She was briefed that she would be walking the casinos carpets to get my money. She started complaining and whining about how she was tired and didn't want to do it. I took this opportunity to pimp hard on her ass and went zip zap crazy and said, "Bitch I don't give a fuck what yo problem is, you gone do what the fuck I tell you to and get yo ass out there and get me my muthafuckin money!" Feeling liberated or some shit she said defiantly, "I'm tired daddy and I ain't got to do nothing if I don't want to!" For trying me I reached back and slapped fire from her face. She sat there shocked and grabbed her jaw. I grabbed her by her hair and started shaking the shit out of her head. I was shaking her like a Pitbull shakes another dog in a dog fight and said, "Bitch I done invested all this time and money in yo muthafuckin hoe ass and you got the nerve to tell me what you ain't gone do. Bitch I own you this is my titties, my ass, and my fuckin pussy, bitch do you hear me? I'll cut your muthafuckin face off if you ever tell me some shit like that again!" Diamond cried and pleaded for me to stop but fuck that I didn't. She ended up being the recipient of all my frustration that I was feeling. I was mad as hell thinking about investing all that money to move out here and on her mom and kid, plus not making any money for a week. I was seething mad. She said apologetically, "Daddy I'm sorry I'm sorry she yelled and cried out. I won't do it again I won't do it again daddy please stop your pulling out my hair!" I was seeing red and said, "I don't give a fuck bitch!" Then I got a hold of myself and calmed down. I was breathing heavily, chest rising and falling with the look of a mad man and said, "Yo momma was right about you, now straighten up this muthafuckin room you ungrateful ass bitch!" She scurried away from me. With her hair all wild and sticking out like the professor on back to the future, she started cleaning up the hotel room immediately. The next week after I gave Diamond **a checkup from the neck up** we made six thousand dollars. "See bitch?" While I'm counting the money I said, "You just have to keep your spirits up. Look at this six G's we made hoeing in these casinos ain't that bad huh?" Acting as if she found religion she says, "Yeah daddy you were right, I like hoeing in the casinos because it's a lot safer and you can see how much a trick is working with right off the top." I saved the money that she made and only spent enough for food and to keep Diamond looking pretty. One day, I was checking out the aesthetics in the hotel area, and some undercover policemen drove up in unmarked cars like thirty cars deep. They jumped out with their guns drawn and looked at me like they knew who I was, but they ran right past me. They surrounded a door and was yelling for the occupant of the hotel to come out with his hands up. I stood by and watched the police do their sting from a small distance, wishing that I had had some popcorn. The occupant either wasn't there or acted as if he wasn't. The police pulled out a small batter ram. Hitting it against the door busting it open and halfway knocking it off its hinges. "Freeze muthafucka freeze!!" The police said as they ran inside the hotel to get my new pimp patna Smooth out and his hands in cuffs. He was wearing some shorts, a T-shirt, and some slides. He was walking with his head down and his mushroom styled perm looked like he was in a cat fight. I didn't know why they did all this for him, but I was spooked now, and I was going to be extra careful now.

45
CHAPTER
❖
YOU REAPED WHAT YOU SOWED

The next night Diamond was looking hella good and as soon as we stepped foot in the casino. She got approached by three different tricks one after another. She called me on her cellphone with happiness not knowing which one she should take first and I said, "Bitch take the one who looks like he gots the most money and is at the nearest hotel." She left and went with the second customer. When she got to his hotel, he explained to her that he wanted her for about 6 hours and if she could give him a good price. She agreed to give him a five-hundred-dollar discount and would only charge him fifty-five hundred for the 6 hours. He said he had been gambling all-night and all he has is poker chips, and if she was willing to still date him and cash them in after his time was up. Dude also stated that he would be willing to tip her at least a thousand dollars. She then thought for a minute, then called me to see if it was cool. I signed off on that shit and gave her a green light to work the sex exchange for the poker chips and I told her that, I'd be at the hotel until she gets done. Man, the trick had his way with her. He was making her do everything under the sun for his money. She was giving me and the trick her best. She wanted to impress me and get all of his money…for us. After his 6 hours were up, he paid her in the Las Vegas casino chips. He also gave her the extra thousand-dollar tip as he promised, and he walked her down to the hotel lobby of his hotel and checked out at the same time. She called me and stood out front of the casino excited about making so much fucking money in one lump sum from one trick. Pulling up to pick her up, hell I was excited too! This is the first time that she had made so much at once and things were starting to pick up for me. "Hey daddy" she said getting into the car and handing over the casino chips. I causally responded, "What's up bitch did you have fun?" Not listening for a response from her. I observed the chips

141

that were in stacks of a hundred dollars and five hundred dollars printed on them and started counting. "We might as well cash these muthafucka's in now and get the money," I said. After we parked the rental car in the parking lot of the casino, we got out and walked through the hotel casino to go to the cashier's booth. That money was burning a hole in my hands, and I had to hurry up and get to the cashier. We stood in line and waited patiently until it was our turn to exchange the casino chips into green currency. Ultimately, we got up to the caged both and started handing the cashier the casinos chips. The lady in the booth paused and said, "Is this some kind of joke Mr. do you really think I'm dumb enough to except these chips as casinos chips and give you cash in return?" I was flabbergasted and responded, "What do you mean isn't that your job ain't that what the fuck you're supposed to do?" I'm light weight getting heated because I thought that this lady was trying to do some racist shit. She responded in a matter-of-fact tone and said, "Yeah, it's my job, and what I'm supposed to do is make sure that the **chips** are real and not the **souvenir chips** you buy at the gift shop for 25 cents apiece!" Diamond and I looked at the cashier lady, and back at the fake casino chips, and both of our hearts sank to the floor. Trying not to look like a fool and keep my respect as much as possible I said, "These casino chips aren't real?" The lady said, "No sir, these chips aren't real you can get them at any gift shop in Las Vegas for 25cents a piece and 6 for a dollar. Feeling herself, the cashier said with a "I was right all along" look on her face, "Do I need to call security?" Hell naw that wouldn't be necessary, and we got up outta there. The cashier could tell that something was wrong with us because we both were visible shaken. The cashier knew that somebody ran a scam game on us and said, "Welcome to Las Vegas honey" with a smirk on her face and yelled "NEXT CUSTOMER PLEASE!". We walked back through the casino looking for the trick that ran the scam on us even though Diamond told me that dude had checked out when he walked her downstairs to the lobby after they finished. She started to cry, and I said, "what did dude look like?" She stated that he was a white boy, dirty blonde, medium build, and in his thirties. He was the surfer type. I was embarrassed and pissed at myself for not giving her a heads up on this part of the game. Hell, to tell you the truth, I didn't get the memo about niggas doing some scandalous shit like that so how could I warn her? Anyway, I said, "Fuck it bitch we've been conned" and headed back to the car pissed off and the both of us quiet as hell. Diamond was extremely upset and rightfully so. We arrived at the car, and she started sobbing uncontrollably. She sat there with tears streaming down her face, as they fell in silence all the way to the hotel. I thought to myself that *a one-thousand-dollar tip didn't sound right from the beginning.* If you were willing to tip so much, then why haggle over the hourly pay? My antennas should've been going off like crazy to even allow us to get played like that. I felt bad for her because, for 6 whole hours, the trick had her and ain't no telling what he had her doing thinking she was about to get fifty-five hundred dollars plus a thousand-dollar tip. I guess that is "poetic justice" for how we robbed that john on our last trip up here when I was pretending to be her estranged husband. I rubbed her shoulders letting her know it was going to be alright. She had taken a shower and washed the day off her body finally. She continued to cry in silence all the way until she fell asleep. For this to happen to us, we for real sowed what we reaped.

46
CHAPTER
✦
STING

The next day we get up and get some lunch in us to be ready for another day of prime time. I could see that her spirits were back to normal from the fiasco last night. Primetime came, and we were back at it again. We both agreed that we are not letting anything get in our way on the road to riches. She was looking extra hoeish like the night before last. I remembered how she was approached by three different tricks at once. I took her back to the same casino that we went to last night hoping that she would attract the same number of customers as she did before. Twenty minutes passed inside the casino when Diamond was approached by a trick, who seemed to be a good catch. Everything went cool as usual, and they headed towards the elevator where the trick had a room to stay. He told her that he had a room on the 22nd floor, but when they entered the elevator three other men came in behind them and the trick pushed the button on the elevator to go to the basement. When Diamond noticed this, she said nervously, "I thought you had a room on the 22nd floor? Why are we going to the basement?" Not knowing what to expect she was ready to fight! She'd be dam if another trick played her like the night before or even attempted to handle her wrong. The trick said, "don't worry ma'am it's just standard procedure." Looking confused she said, "Standard procedure, what the fuck you mean standard procedure?" She started reaching into her purse to pull out the mase that had a loud horn on it so when you pulled it, the horn would blow for ten minutes. When the trick saw her reaching, he whipped out his gun and told her not to even think about using that dam thing on him or he would be forced to use his weapon. She didn't know what type of freaky shit they were planning on doing with her against her will down in the basement and she was petrified. She froze when she saw the weapon. The other three gentleman spoke saying, "Ma'am you are being arrested for prostitution in the city and state of Las Vegas Nevada." All the gentlemen pulled out their badges and showed them to her briefly and put them back inside their jacket pockets. At first, she was relieved, but then she thought about it and asked, "Why me?" She broke down and started crying. They finally reached the basement in the casino and the police officers put handcuffs on her, frisked her, and checked her purse. They proceed to put her in the back of the police car and drove her to the Las Vegas City Jail. While she was getting fingerprinted, they made her take her tracks out of her hair and break her nails off. They told her she was allowed one phone call and to hurry up. She called me but got no answer, and she was so upset and scared she didn't leave a message. Meanwhile I was waiting for Diamond to finish her date and I tried my luck at the crap table again. losing about five hundred dollars before I looked and realized that my phone was ringing. It was a blocked number, so I wasn't tripping off of it, so I didn't bother to answer. I just rolled the dice and continued to try and win back the money I had lost. After losing fifteen hundred I pried myself away from the crap table to go sweat a few bitches on the track. Something ain't right? *Normally she checks in with a brutha.* I said to myself, "Dam this bitch ain't called me to check in or none of the shit, she must be really having a good time with that muthafuckin trick she's with." *Let me call this hoe and make sure everything is everything.* I dialed Diamonds' cellphone; I got no answer. Starting to get worried now, I left the casino and walked the track in hopes of finding her. I came up empty, no sight of Diamond anywhere. I made my way to the hotel where we were staying at, and I sat down to think for a minute. All kinds of assumptions came in my head. *I hope nobody slipped her a 'mickey' and she is laid out somewhere. Did she decide not to fuck with me anymore? Did she choose another pimp? Did she get the money from the trick and split and go back home to her mother and child? Has something terrible happened to her?* As my mind was racing, I asked myself, "*Dam where the fuck is this bitch?*" At that time my phone ranged from a restricted number again, this time I picked it up. I said, "Yeah?" sounding concerned and scared she said, "Daddy?" I immediately "went ham" on her and lit into her ass for not calling and checking in with me. "Bitch where the fuck you at?" Why you ain't answering your phone and why are you calling me from a restricted number?" She yelled and cut me off and said, "I'm in jail daddy, that last trick you saw me with was an undercover cop!" After she told me that, I fucking slouched on the couch." I said, "Dam baby, is that right?" I had a funny feeling about his ass when I saw him again in the casino with another bitch. I started to walk up on his ass and ask if he had seen you, but something told me not to do it. She hurried up and said, "Daddy I met this other hoe in jail that hooked me up with a three way to holla at you." I asked, "How much is your bail?" She took a deep breath and started to cry and said angrily, "They want twenty thousand to get me out, but you only have to pay 10 percent of that. You don't need a bond all you have to do is pay the money and come get me."

Instantly I thought about the money that I had lost at the crap table. Plus, I'm getting low on the cash that I came down here with. I decided not to pay the money to get her out and keep those two gees for living expenses. I said reassuringly, "Alright bitch I'll be down there in a minute to bail you out, let me call to find out where the police station is, and I will be down there to get you." She perked up and said, "Okay daddy!" then I hung up the phone. I knew that Diamond could make the money back, but with all the bad luck we were having, I doubted a little. The good thing was that she has never been in any trouble before. Prostitution is a misdemeanor and I hoped that she would get out of jail when she got arranged at her court date. If she didn't, I would go ahead and pay the money to get her out. The next morning, I was still sleeping soundly, and was awakened by my cellphone ringing. I figured it was Diamond calling to see when and why I haven't bailed her out yet. After about ten minutes it rang again with the same restricted I.D caller calling. This kept up for about an hour until I said, fuck it and picked it up. "Yeah" I answered slightly agitated. "Daddy I'm out of jail!" Diamond proceeded to tell me exactly about how she got caught up in the sting operation. Everything from the men in the elevator to the police that rode with her to the basement. She asked cautiously and respectfully, "How come you wasn't answering the phone?" I quickly said, "The phone was in the car where I left it at last night." As I'm wiping the sleep out of my eye I asked her, "How did you get out?" She happily exclaimed, "They gave me an order release on the terms that I show up at my first court date on my own terms." Knowing the real reason I didn't answer the phone is because, I was going to let her sit it out and wait until the courts let her go. "Anyway, I'm on my way."

47
CHAPTER
❖
HOE EASY COME HOE EASY GO

Diamond and I went to her first court date. The judge told her she was banned from the main casinos for 8 years, and if she caught another hoe case, she would be put in jail. Everything worked out cool, even though she was banned from the main casinos in Vegas, she could still walk the track and hoe in different casinos. I came across a casino that was cool and bumped into a security guard that said he would take money under the table to let Diamond hustle in there freely without any problems. After a while I put two and two together and I knew that's why the other hoes were able to hoe in those main casinos and not get sweated. Wishing that I would've known then what I know now, maybe Diamond wouldn't have had a hoe case and get banned from the main strip. Moving on, now with the escort service, and the track, and the plug at the casinos, I was making some good money. The game was finally making Diamond and I smile again. One day she had called and said that she has another date lined up as usual. After about two hours I hadn't heard from her, and I started to get suspicious. Now I was getting nervous thinking that maybe she got caught up with another case. Suddenly my phone started ringing and relieved I answered, "Bitch is you alright?" Responding back like she had some "tea" to tell me. She said lowly, "Yeah daddy I'm cool, I came across this cop I thought was a trick." He told me he liked the way I was conducting myself out here on the track. The cop gave me the game on the laws of entrapment. Now that I have that understanding daddy, there is no way ever that I should catch another hoe case! Plus, he said when he is out here, I don't have anything to worry about and that he would tell his fellow officers to leave me alone. I would've been called and told you, but I wanted to give him my undivided attention." Looking surprised and giving her some props, I said, "Dam bitch is that right, things are really starting to look up for us now huh?" Basking in my approval she spryly said, "Yep, and guess what, remember that other hoe I met in jail that hooked me up with that three way to call you?" Not really in the mood to play twenty-one guesses I said, "Yeah bitch I remember, what about her?" Acting like she is asking a parent if it was alright for her friend to spend a night for the sleepover she says, "Well she is out here and said her daddy has left her for dead. She ain't got no place to go, so I thought maybe I could bring her home to you and you could see if you want her on the team or not." She was talking a little bit too much for me and I waved my hand in the air as if I'm swatting gnats and responded, "Yeah bitch that will work, gone ahead and continue doing what you're doing and call me back later." After I disconnected the line without hearing her say goodbye or anything. I waited with great anticipation to meet this newly found prospect and see what she was about. They say every man's garbage is another man's treasure. More hoes means more dollars, so I'm with it! Diamond and the prospect left the track and made it to where I told them to meet me. Diamond already didn't like the bitch, so I asked, "Diamond what the fuck is wrong with you? Why are your lips turned upside down like you been sucking a sour dick or something?" She quickly stated, "Naw daddy it ain't like that, I don't like this bitch already." If I wouldn't have told you I had knocked you a bitch, I would've been beat this bitch ass! Just give me the word and I will stomp on this bitch like Kirk Franklin!" I'm laughing slightly and said, "Well hold up, what's wrong with the bitch?" Seeing that she was clearly agitated and said to me, "I can't really explain daddy, you'll just have to see for yourself." She was standing a few feet away looking like she was unimpressed with me. She was five-foot tall, light skinned, big titties with a belly protruding over her belt, she wore a bronze and blonde wig, cute face with a button noise, a flat ass and a terrible attitude and a sweater dress. Walking towards her I put on my gentleman charm and said, "Hi you doing lil mama?" She was looking so anticlimactic, but I continued and said, "I understand you looking to shake a hand and meet a friend I'm Big Dawg," and extended my hand to give her a handshake. Begrudgingly she shook my hand with an attitude and was acting like she was God's gift to the world and said, "First of all I need to get away from your bitch! I don't know who she thinks she is, trying to tell me how to deal with a pimp. Second of all I need you to take me to get something to eat! Oh yeah and put me in the shower, give me some good dick before I can even think about fuckin with you." I looked at her in awe and switched the gentleman switch, to the gorilla switch. "Bitch first of all you done ran into a rich hoes' nightmare and a poor hoes wet dream, who the fuck you think you talking to in this muthafucka?" Now she had me acting a fool for real and I continued, "You talking bout you hungry, need a shower and want some dick, it sounds like you don't what a pimp, bitch you want a boyfriend!" I grabbed her by her throat and took her purse and ran through her pockets at the same time. "I see why your ex-pimp left your ass for dead. Bitch with your little smart ass mouth its purse first and ass last when you fuck with a nigga like me! Bitch how much money you got on you?" she could barely speak because my hands wrapped around her throat so tight. I let her stupid ass go and managed to get three hundred and seventy-five dollars out of her and put it in my dam pocket. Angrily I said, "Bitch you stay in a hoes place when you talking to a pimp, and if you ever get out of pocket again Ima slap yo ass so hard your head will spin." The hoe that Diamond brought to me sat there stunned. She had never been dealt with in this kind of manner before. She broke down and started to cry. I was like fuck it and stayed in gorilla mode saying, "Ah naw hell naw, you cry baby ass bitch I don't need yo ass in my stable cause one bad apple will fuck up the rest of em." I turned my wrath to Diamond and asked, "Why did you bring me this ole emotional broke ass bitch?" Graciously and nervously, she responded, "I was just trying to bring you another bitch to help us get to the top daddy, I didn't know she was gone turn out to be a punk bitch." Accepting her reply I said, "Well come on bitch let's leave this pathetic ass hoe and get up out of here before this hoe gets us caught up." We left that hoe and jumped in the car laughing headed home. Hoe easy come, and hoe easy go.

48
CHAPTER
❖
THE ROOSTER COMES TO REST

Christy, Diamonds mother sent a kite telling us that we needed to come home because her son was hella sick. She left a message saying that his temperature was 105. Of course, we dropped everything and came back to Cali. Arriving at her Aunties house and banging on the door. We find that Blaxton is safe and sound and eating top ramen and shit. Diamonds Auntie answers the door like is everything okay? Diamond chimes in and says that my mother sent an urgent message about the baby. Auntie just leaned her head to the side and took a deep breath. Auntie is in her early fifties, colorful head rag on, with lime green sweatpants and an oversized white tee. You could tell she used to be something back in her day. She always has a cigarette in between her two fingers, head always tilted to the side and her attitude is fuck off. Auntie gave us the real reason for the message, and it was because she kicked her free loading sister Christy out. Turns out that all that time that we were sending money back home for the baby. Her mother was pocketing the money and buying new clothes and getting her hair and nails done. Diamond was furious and she proclaimed that she would beat the shit out of her mother for pulling a stunt like that. She was going to wait until her mother parks her car in the Aunties parking spot and get her. After about two and a half hours Diamond came running into the house to grab her shoes and a bat. Auntie and I knew what time it was. Auntie stopped her and said, "Bitch I know you ain't gone use no bat to beat your momma up, are you?" I know she a lazy ass fuck and all but that's still my sister." With a reassuring secretive tone Diamond says, "Naw the bitch in the car sleep. I'm gonna scare the shit out the bitch and bust her dam windshield out then drag her ass out the car and beat the shit out of her." She said with a demented smile. I was going to tell her not to bust the windshield out but to bust one of the side windows out instead, but it was too late. All you heard was a big crash, crash, crash and Diamond was on top of her mother's hood swinging away cursing like hell. Christy jumped out of her sleep scared to death. When she saw that it was her daughter, she didn't even want to open the car door to see what her problem was because, she already knew. Diamond seething with this demented smile mixed with a rage look on her face demanded that she opened the car door. She told her mother to get out or she would bust out the back window and all of the side windows. "Christy was looking for sympathy from me, but I kept chewing my toothpick and turned my head away. Ready to face the inevitable, she opened her car door and before she could even put her foot out, Diamond was all over her like a piranha! Diamond was grabbing her by her hair pulling it and throwing punches with her other hand. By Diamond being so small and in shape from walking and fucking all the time on the strip, and her mother being a rotund fat ass bitch, she was able to move around and jump on her mother. It wasn't even a contest. Her mother was defenseless and squealing for help! She was so petrified she wasn't even trying to fight her back. From the way the fight was going and how brave Diamond was and how scared her mother was that this wasn't there first fight. I couldn't take the sight any longer and stepped in to grab Christy yelling, "That's enough, that's enough. I realized that I had grabbed the wrong person, because Diamond saw this as an impression for free punches and kept whopping her mother's ass, going around me. I told Diamond, "Bitch I ain't gone tell you again," when she noticed the fierceness in my voice then she stopped because she knew I may end up slapping her for not listening to me. But that didn't stop her from cussing up a storm and ranting and raving. Christy's hair was all over the ground, her clothes were torn, and she had different places where blood was coming from. Blood came from her lip, nose, and she had scratches on her face that Diamond gave her. Her nails were broken, and blood coming from them as well. Christy was sobbing and was trying to plead with me saying how sorry she was and how crazy her daughter was. Then she threatened to call the police on Diamond when she looked in her side mirror and saw all the damage that she did. When I heard the word police, I got myself in action and grabbed Diamond and led the way up to her auntie's house. I gave her auntie a hundred for the baby and said from now on I would send the money directly to her. Diamond hugged and kissed her baby, and all he said was, "leave me alone bitch" because he had no idea what was going on. She told him she loved him too and we left her aunt's house in a hurry. I wanted to go see my family but decided not to with Christy calling the police on us I didn't want to chance it. Ain't no telling what she would tell them out of spite. So, I bounced and got us a hotel room and headed back to Las Vegas the next day.

49
CHAPTER
❖❖
THE BEAT DOWN

Meanwhile back at aunties house, Christy was still devastated about what her daughter did to her. She had revenge on her mind in the worst way. Not only did her daughter beat her down to a pulp, but she wrecked her car. Replaying what had just happened in her mind and that's what made her upset the most. Good thing I stopped her from beating her down any worse because she may have had to take a trip to the emergency room. Days later auntie gave me the information about the aftermath concerning the beat down. Christy sat in her car after she got herself together in her sister's house and thought of the worse ways, she could get back at her daughter for what she did. She started by calling the police and filing an assault and battery police report. "This is 911 emergency how may I direct your call?" said the operator. "Um I would like to speak with the Police Department Division, I have been beaten very badly and want to file a complaint," said Christy. "Hold please," said the operator. She held or for a few minutes hearing the phone ring a dozen times finally a voice picked up and said, "This is Officer Pavlock of the Oakland Police Department how my I help you?" Christy said, "I would like to file a complaint and press full charges on a person who vandalized my vehicle and assaulted me. The Officer said, "OK mam were there one or more persons who assaulted you?" Crying she answered, "Two persons sir." Even though I had no parts of it and stopped Diamond from literally beating the shit out of her, she knew her daughter wouldn't be able to survive without my help. She was trying to destroy her in hopes of being back homeless and man less like herself. The Officer said, "O.K. ma'am give me your location and I will come and file the complaint for you." She gave the Officer her address and waited in her car until he arrived. He pulled up in his squad car and located Christy in her car waiting. He got out and introduced himself ready to file a report on her behalf. Instantly Christy started running at the mouth saying how we had beat her up and damaged her car. When Christy said my name, the officer stopped writing with his pen and said, "Big Dawg with the Expedition truck?" Fastly, agreeing she said, "Yeah, that's him but he lost his Expedition to a bail bondsman behind some hoe he had bailed out of jail who never showed up to court." Officer Pavlock said, "Well this case will be a personal thing for me now. I need to question him about a murder that happened concerning one of his workers by the name of Dave-baby." He continued with a devilish smile and said, "I had an informant who told me that Big Dawg may have had something to do with it." She looked at him flabbergasted with her hand covering her mouth and said, "Well I don't know anything about no murder but, I know he's a pimp." Christy continued, "They don't stay up this way anymore, him and my daughter have moved down to Las Vegas. He is pimping on her somewhere down there." The son of a bitch held me while my daughter beat me up. He had the nerve to get a bat and started busting out the windshield on my car. My daughter is a prostitute and neglects her child and does nothing for him. If it wasn't for me taking care of my daughter's child, he would be in a foster home or group home somewhere. She beat me up because I wouldn't give her any money and I wouldn't give her her child back. I have full custody of him, and I wasn't going to put him in danger by being with his mother. While lying through her teeth she continued to bash and belittle us. Luckily auntie had heard some of the lies and tried to vouch for us. Christy continued to play the roll and said, "I want them charged for assault and battery and put in jail!" Taking notes and eating up all of her lies, Officer Pavlock wrote down all the things Christy told him and said, "Don't worry ma'am, we'll issue a warrant for their arrests." The officer personally says, "I'll get down to the bottom of this, the only thing is I can't issue a worldwide warrant for an assault. I can only issue a statewide warrant for their arrest." Smiling behind his dark shades looking like the feds he says, "They will have to come to California to face charges and questioning of the murder when they get here." With her arm folded and a head nod for confirmation about what's going to happen to them she says, "That sounds like a plan to me Officer." He happily gives her his card to keep in touch in case she has further news about their whereabouts. Auntie told me that she politely declined his card and walked away. Diamond's mother not yet finished, was thinking of another way to get back at her daughter. Auntie told me that she chastised her sister for being so evil. Christy's response was oh yeah, well watch this. She pulled out her cellphone and started dialing. The person on the other line sounding unenthused says, "This is the Child Protective Service of Alameda County how may I help you?" Acting as if she was trying to get an Oscar, she sounds like a concerned citizen and says, "I would like to report a child neglection report." She told the case worker how Diamond neglects her child and is abusive to him. She added the fact that she was a prostitute and has a pimp who abuses the baby. She stated that she leaves the baby at her aunt's house for months at a time because she has no place to stay. The case worker wanted to verify who Christy was to Diamond and she said she would rather remain anonymous. The case worker asked where the aunts house was located so they could send out a private investigator to do some investigating and Christy, obliged. Now Christy sat in her car satisfied because diamond had the police to worry about, and Child Protective Services to worry about. Auntie told me that her sister is dead wrong for this, but her hands were tied.

50
CHAPTER
❖
A DREAM DEFERRED

Meanwhile driving back to Vegas with me Diamond says, "Daddy I'm ready to get back out on the track and hoe, I'm ready to get some money." Appreciating her eagerness I said, "Bitch you needs to calm down and get yourself together and regroup before you get back out there on the track." Since we been down here I ain't had a chance to do any research about my trucking company to see if I can find any contractors who are looking for owner operators. So, we gone kick back for a week or two and enjoy the fruits of our labor while I try to see who is hiring. "You do realize what we are doing is illegal don't you?" I don't plan for us to be doing this shit forever. In agreement she stated, "O.K. daddy I'm just telling you I'm struggling to be that ideal hoe that keeps you paid under any circumstances." I grabbed the Las Vegas newspaper and went to the want ads. Finding a few leads, I started scribbling down some contractors looking to hire truck operators. After placing a few calls, a couple of interviews were set up for the following day. It was frustrating because so far, every interview that I went to everyone slammed the door in my face due to lack of experience. Also, I didn't own a truck yet. Suddenly I had an epiphany, *truckers are some of the biggest tricks in the game.* My next interview I will have Diamond dress nice and hoeish and bring her with me to see if I can catch a contractor's eye with her by my side. The next interview that I went to I had Diamond by my side, and finally I found a contractor who believed in me. The contractor that I found couldn't keep is eyes off Diamond. He was so star struck by her appearance that he would stutter and answer my questions with an incoherent response. Laughing on the inside *I thought I saw foam start to build up in the corner of his mouth.* After the interview was over, I signed a contract that stated the contractor would put me through a Big Rig Truck Buyers Purchase Program. The program would let me put down a payment of five thousand on my first Big Rig Truck. The job would pay me to transport metal locally and pay is four thousand a week. We shook hands to seal the business deal and we left the construction site and headed back to the house. I was pulling up to the contractor's work site. An undercover cop put on his sirens and pulled me over. He got on his loudspeaker causing a scene and told me to shut off my engine and to throw the keys out the window. The undercover cop got out of his car with his gun drawn on Diamond and I and approached the car with caution. By this time, I could see that my contractor was looking from the work site wondering what was going on. I was scared shit-less thinking I was going to jail for some bullshit and going to be extradited back to California for the questioning of a murder. When the undercover cop got to my side window he said, "I pulled you over because you were speeding and swerving your car from lane to lane. Give me your license and registration." At first, I was about to argue with this fool because if that was the case, why would you have your gun drawn on us like that. Ole scary ass nigga, I pulled out my information and pointed over to the work site and told the undercover cop that I was on my way to work. I was in a hurry and talking on the cellphone which is described as **distracted driving** and that was the reason for me speeding and swerving. I told him that I apologize for making him do his job. He just looked at me in an unbelieving way and said, "Let me run a check on you to make sure you don't have any warrants and if you come back clean, I will let you off with a warning." I sat there with sweat running down my forehead thinking the worst as the undercover cop took thirty minutes to run me through the system. He walked back to the car and told me to step out. This was a for sure way to embarrass me at my new job. The undercover cop said, "Have you guys been drinking?" as he looked at me square in my eyes to see if the pupils were dilated. Firmly I said, "No officer I don't drink or do any drugs." The officer smirked to himself knowing I was lying, "Well I'm going to perform a sobriety test on you, and if you pass, I will let you go. If you fail, you're going to get a ticket for Driving Under the Influence. I was upset but was still glad he didn't have anything on me, and I knew that I had been drinking a little bit earlier. He did the tests on me, and I failed as he knew I would. He told me to get back in my car and that he was going to write the D.U.I ticket. Sitting in my car looking over at the worksite, and I saw the look of concern on the contractors' face. Knowing that this whole scene was bad for business I shook my head in disgust. The undercover cop brought me the D.U.I. ticket and told me that if I was in California, he could've taken me to jail for Driving Under the Influence. Since I was in Nevada all he could do was give me a ticket. "Please sign on the dotted line sir." I took the pen out of the undercover's cop hand and signed my name. He gave me my copy, he took the original for himself, and told me to have a nice day and walked back to his car. I waited for him to leave, then I got my car keys off the ground and started the car. The contractor motioned me to come back to the work site. Soon as I got out the car, the contractor walked up and said, "Why did that cop pull you over?" Looking puzzled I said, "I don't know, he was just being a dick head." I was jokingly trying to push pass the awkwardness and he said, "Well I saw him giving you a sobriety test, then he gave you a ticket. Is the ticket for Driving Under the Influence?" I wanted to lie so bad and say that it wasn't but as soon as the contractor ran my license, he would find out any way. So, I said, "Yeah man he did, is this going to affect my driving privileges as a trucker for your company?" Without hesitation he answered, "I'm afraid it is, the insurance is going to be too high for me to cover you, plus your license will be suspended as a class A truck driver for at least 2 or 3 years. I'm sorry I'm going to have to terminate the contract we negotiated on." Man, I couldn't believe my ears. I went to truck driving school, paid the cash to attend, moved down to Vegas thinking that would be better for my trucking business. With all my blood, sweat, and tears I went through to get a contract, saved up plenty of money, all to have my dream ruined in a hours' time. At this point I felt despair. "I understand Sir" I said to the man who was going to employ me. When I get this all taken care of in the next few years I'll come back and look you up!" Shaking his head in agreement but he knew that I would never see him again he said, "You sure can, and it will be a pleasure to give you another chance. If it will help you any, I have 3 D.U.I.'s on my record and look at me now, and I'm 50 years old. I'm a success in the trucking industry, but I had to take my lumps and bruises like everybody else. We are truck drivers, and most of us aren't saints. We have criminal records long as Las Vegas Blvd. Your only nineteen years old, so you still have a lot of growing up to do. If I told you what else was on my record you wouldn't even believe it. So just because you ran into at what seems like a dead end, don't get discouraged, keep pushing to conquer your dreams. Take it from me, I know." At once I said, "Thanks Sir, for the words of encouragement, I needed that." Well, you will be hearing from me, and I wish you the best Sir." He said, "Thank you son" and I rode off the work site feeling motivated with even more ambition from the contractor's lecture.

51
CHAPTER
❖
THREES A CROWD

Diamond's phone started to ring, and she realized it was her auntie. Looking concerned she says, "Hey auntie how's my baby?" Getting straight to the point she says, "The baby is fine girl, but it's the people you gone have to worry about." Looking puzzled Diamond says, "What people?" Auntie sounding as if she is looking around so that nobody hears her and says, "Those Child Protective Services people who yo mamma called and told them all kinds of lies about you and the baby's livelihood." Sounding a little bit rattled she continues to say, "They sent a private investigator to my house and tried to take the baby from me." Diamond scrunched up her face and asked, "Are you serious auntie?" Trying to get through to her she said, "Yes girl yes, may God be my witness!" I had to keep him standing in the doorway and lie to him and say I don't know what he is talking about, and don't know baby stay here. After I denied all of that, Blaxton toys and diaper bags were sitting in the hallway right next to the doorway." The bastard looked at Blaxton's stuff and looked me in the eyes and said, "If a baby doesn't stay here, then who's belongings is this in the hallway?" I couldn't think of a quick enough response, and he said, "I'll be back with a search warrant from the county." He smiled at me while wearing them matrix type glasses and turned around and left me standing there with my mouth hanging wide open. "You better hurry up and pick up the baby before these people get back and take him away from you." This time we didn't drive back to California I bought two tickets at the airport on the first thing headed back to the bay area. While on the airplane Diamond was a nervous wreck. She was fidgety and couldn't stop moving and rightfully so. The only thought in her mind was her baby and what if the Child Protective Services got to him before we arrived. I was in deep thought my dam self, thinking about *how deceitful her mother Christy was and if she had done anything else out of revenge toward her daughter.* I thought of a million and one things she could do but I figured only time would tell. This went on all the way until we reached auntie's house and got out the cab. Diamond knocked on her aunt's door with non-stop with aggression. "Diamond is that you?" her auntie said not being able to see because she had no peep hole on her door. "Yes, auntie it's me, did the Child Protective Services people come take my baby?" Auntie speaking up a little bit said, "Hell naw they ain't came and took the baby," she said as she opened the door. Auntie intrepidly continued on to say, "They would have to use a battering-ram and drag me to the county jail before I let them just come in here and take this baby!" As the auntie hurries us inside and peeps behind us to see if anyone was watching and says, "That's why I didn't answer the door until I figured out it wasn't the private investigator." Blaxton was sitting in the living room with a plate full of top ramen noodles and hot dogs looking at cartoon network station. The baby paid no attention to us as he sat looking at T.V. without a care in the world. We had to hurry up and pack up little man shit and bounce back to Vegas. Finally, the cab arrived, and Diamond wrapped the baby up like he was newborn, and I took all of his things, and we ran to the cab loading it up in a hurry. When we were finished, auntie started to shed a few tears telling the baby that she loves him and how she would miss him. I dug in my pocket and offered auntie a few hundred dollars, but she declined it, I figured hell she was the one that should've received the money because she was actually taking care of little man. While she was trying her best not to break down and cry in front of us, she said, "Y'all be careful and take care of my baby," as she closed the apartment door. The cab driver then drove off and dropped us off at the airport quickly. Everything went cool and we bounced on the airplane back to Vegas without any problems. When we made it back to Las Vegas and arrived home, I studied Diamond and her son as she fed him his favorite top ramen noodles and hot dogs. "Dam, I thought to myself, *I done fucked around and inherited a dam family.* How come on those pimp D.V.D.'s they don't tell you shit like this? What if something happens to this bitch, she can end up going to jail, get stabbed by a trick and end up dead or all kinds of shit. Can I deal with this kind of shit on my conscience if something like that happens? I would hate to be the reason something happens to Blaxton's mother not being there in his life… dam. I needed her undivided attention and said, "A bitch let me talk to you for a minute." Willingly she says, "OK daddy let me put the cartoon network on for the baby and I'll be right there." I started to say bitch when I said let me talk to you for a minute that means now! But I couldn't because now, her baby came first. So, I would have to also put the baby before the pimpin. When she finished getting her son settled in and came to my attention I said, "Look lil-momma, I don't want you to feel obligated or pressured to be in the game with me. You know the consequences just like I do. If you decide that you don't want to do this anymore, it doesn't mean I won't continue to be your friend." But before I could finish my speech, she interrupted me and said, "Daddy, I want you to be the best pimp ever. I want you to shine I don't care what happens to me, I do and don't care if I got to go to jail, get rapped, or none of that shit, I just want to be able to say I was the one who helped you get to the top and was the downiest bitch you ever had in your life." While she was saying this, tears started to water in her eyes, and rolled down her cheeks. Dabbing her tears with the top of her hand she says, "Just promise me that if something bad happens to me that you will take care of my baby and I will die for you daddy." I looked at her almost as if she was another woman and remembered what Nina had told me over the phone before I left California to move to Vegas. "I don't think you realize how much power you possess over people is what Nina had told me." Starting to feel a little bit emotional, but I knew that I couldn't show it and said, "Lil-momma I promise don't worry about Blaxton. If something happens, I will take care of him with all my might as if he was my own." Then I beckoned for her to come and hug me. I ain't gone lie, I hugged her in the living room for about 10 minutes not letting her go until she finished crying. Out of all the women that I had in my life, no one has ever said that they would take the consequence of death for me. I figured that now was the time to take this to another level. I had never had sex with Diamond since I met her because I was sticking to the script of manipulation. I led her to the bedroom and we both took a shower together. When we both got out, I did the unbelievable to her. I gave her one of my pussy eating, asshole, and toes licking, marathon fucking for three and a half hours straight with no breaks. After we finished having good sex, I left her in the room to sleep and walked in the living room and checked on Blaxton. He was still looking at T.V. not looking like he moved an inch.

52
CHAPTER

❖

UNBELIEVABLE

After my pimp patna Smooth got out of jail, he was hurting for money and hoes. He and I went to the casinos to try and knock a few bitches. Lil-Pimp went back to the town to regroup, so our faction just became a dynamic duo. No Diamond with me tonight, just the fellas doing what we do. Some pimps would greet him and listen to his story and walk away laughing at him behind his back. I realized then that these niggas were out here giving fake luv. They weren't honoring the fraternity code of ethics for pimping. Smooth just shook his head like a batter being called on a third strike and said, "You see Big Dawg?" he continued to say, "All these niggas act like they're my friends, and as soon as I ask them for a couple of dollars, they act like they ain't got it. That's how I know you are a genuine dude. You barley even know me, and you're out here looking out for a nigga." I said, "Smooth man, I come from the streets before I was doing this pimpin I was on the block selling coke. I know how it is to have a patna who is less fortunate than me whose momma smoke crack, or pops ain't around to help. I know how it is when a nigga was doing good in the game and fell off. It happened to me plenty of times, but I would still strive in the game and try to get back what I lost with interest. That's what I like about you man. You're not giving up, most niggas would've fell on their face and squared up. That's why I'm going to help you get back on your feet. I admire your determination." Looking appreciative he responded to me, "Thanks Big Dawg," the game God is sure going to bless you when it's your turn to receive his blessings!" What I just told Smooth was more of a reason for him to prove his loyalty to me. We continued to walk down the Las Vegas Strip in search for hoes, then decided to go into one of the casinos. We went in and decided to go to the bar and have a few drinks. Even though me and Smooth were both underage we didn't look it, and never got carded for I.D. I paid for the drinks, and we just talked about what goes down in Las Vegas and the pimp game in general. Suddenly, we heard a commotion of people yelling and screaming then we heard a lot of high-powered rifles and semi-automatic handguns shooting. We from **the town** so we ducked for cover and got out of the way. People were falling over each other running so fast and trampling over people who had fallen to the ground. There were crap tables being pushed over, card tables being slung to the ground, and people were knocking over the slot machines. The shots rang out for about five long minutes and people were being gunned down from stray bullets. The scene was chaotic and gore. After the shooting we both said, "Let's get the fuck out of here!" Smooth said "Hold on a minute Big Dawg this type of shit always happens in Vegas. This is the perfect opportunity for me to pick up some of these money chips that fell off these playing tables." Looking like the devil came over him, Smooth, dashed to were one of the crap tables had fallen and immediately started picking up money chips off the ground. People were so scared they didn't dare pick up any chips and continued to run and scream. He picked up as many chips as he could before the police were on the scene to gain control of the situation. I came from cover, and we ran through the casino to the exit doors. Breathing tirelessly, I said in between breaths, "Dam did you see that shit, it was people laying on the ground with bullet holes in them and muthafucka's getting kicked and trampled over and blood all over that muthafucka?" Getting his jog on while smiling about his quick come up he said, "Yeah man that's how it be down here a lot when the Crip and Bloods be coming thru here. This is the third time this shit has happened since I been staying down here," he said nonchalantly as he counted his chips and walked down the street calmly. He looked up and said to me, "Here you go Big Dawg this is your cut of the money chips I just came up on" and handed me ten gees worth of chips. Smiling with satisfaction he was putting the other ten thousand in his pockets. Smooth said, "Oh that was the "game God" right there, giving us some of those blessings you were telling me about." I just cracked a smile and said, "That's how pimp patnas in crime do it in Sin City we share the trap money and keep on pimpin!" After that come up, we became the pimp patnas in crime.

53
CHAPTER
❖
INNOCENCE TAKEN

Since Diamond and I went to another level to this pimp shit. She wanted to share things with me. I asked her how come she be going at it like that with her mother. Her body language changed, and her shoulders slumped, and she said, "Alright Daddy, I'll tell you the truth." When she was a little girl like pre-adolescent her mother called to her and said, "Baby, come from outside and see what mommies' friend want, he has some candy for you." She came from the front porch playing with her barbie dolls and from doing hopscotch. "Yes, mommy she said to her mother. "Go in the room with my friend and he is going to play doctor on you, and when he finishes, he will give you some candy!" Christy told her. Diamond said, "but I don't want to play doctor with your friend mommy, can I just have the candy anyway?" In an aggressive and agitated way Christy responded, "No, you can't have the fuckin candy you little spoiled bitch! Now get your ass in that room with my friend and don't come out until he is finished playing doctor with your smart mouthed ass!" Christy was eager to get her next hit of crack and that couldn't happen unless her daughter participated with the dealer. Diamond started crying as she went towards the door to enter the room her mother's friend was waiting for her in. When she walked inside the room it was pitch black. She could only see the silhouette of the person but knew he was a grown man and was very large fat and out of shape. Breathing hard and deep you could hear his glee and anticipation about what is getting ready to go down. He says falsely, "It's okay." The heavy-set man pulled her by the hand and led her to the bed. The heavy-set man started undressing her as she stood there crying saying she didn't want to play doctor. He tried to reassure her but that was a lie too and said, "It won't hurt sweetie, now lay on the bed like a good little girl and let me do my check up so this will be over quick, and you can have your candy." Diamond laid on the bed naked still crying while the fat heavy set man, took off his clothes and stroked himself butt-hole naked to get his manhood aroused. She hated reliving what her mother had done to her when she was a nine-years old. Diamond never knew her mother was a crack hoe because by the time she was able to understand what her mother did, she had got herself together and stopped doing drugs. However, she did remember that incident with her mother's fat, nasty, perverted, friend. That was one of the prime reasons she hated her mother so much and disrespected her every chance she got. Reminiscing about what had happened to her made her call her mother in a rage. She threatened to beat her ass the next time she saw laid eyes on her for calling Child Protective Services and spending the money that she was sending to her for the baby. She hadn't found out about her mother calling the police on her and filing a police report on us yet. Or that I was wanted for questioning regarding a homicide that occurred. "Hello?" Christy answered her phone knowing that it was her daughter calling, "You fat ass bitch, how you gone take our problems out on my baby by calling the C.P.S. and put them in our business?" said Diamond. "You put your hands on me and beat me the fuck up in front of your nigga and fucked up my car! You know who much I love my car!" Her mother continued on hurt and angry and said, "You embarrassed me in front of that nigga and made me look like shit. So, I did what I had to do to make your life miserable like mines. Ever since that nigga has been fucking with you, you act like I don't exist. If his ass wasn't around, this shit wouldn't be happening to us. He has corrupted you and turned us against each other. I will be glad when the police snatch you and his ass up and take y'all to jail!" As she leaned into the phone she spewed, "You just jealous!" Diamond shot back. "You want me to be living in my car like you, you don't want me to have a man who actually cares about me and don't just want to fuck me or give him a lap dance! If it wasn't for Big Dawg, we would've been homeless, if it wasn't for him we wouldn't have had time with Blaxton, if it wasn't for him, you wouldn't have rims on that piece of shit car you love so much! That nigga has been good to me, and my baby and you are just an old jealous ass bitch who can't find a man for nothing in the world! And what the fuck you mean when the police snatch our ass up, we ain't did nothing for the police to be looking for us?" Letting the cat out of the bag in a grinch way you could hear her she smile and says, "Well my little darling, after you and Big Dawg left from picking up Blaxton and you whooping my ass, I called the police and filled out a police report on you and him. I told the police that both of you assaulted me and beat the shit out of me. And, while I was filling out the report about what happened, the police officer heard Big Dawg's name and bells started ringing. He said he knew Big Dawg and that he was a dope dealer who was wanted for murder." She continued to sing with more hurtful and damaging things and said, "The officer said that Big Dawg killed a man and left him in his car down the street from where they sold rocks. It happened at a dead in street, and he knows it was Big Dawgs car. I told him you are a whore, and he pimps on you and that y'all have moved down to Las Vegas." Diamond erupted and said, "Bitch, I hate you how could you have done all of this just because we had a fight! We had plenty of fights and you never done no shit like this before, I hate you! You are an evil self-centered ass old bitch! He was the one who helped me from beating yo ass by holding me back, if it wasn't for him, you would've been in a hospital by now! I wish you would fuckin die! You are talking about me a pimp, bitch you the muthafuckin pimp! I remember you had me have sex with a grown ass man when I was a little girl!? I know that man gave you some money or something to have sex with me. That's one of the reasons I am the way I am now is because of you! That's why I am a disrespectful child, that turned into a hoe! I was a hoe before I met Big Dawg in case you forgot bitch, he met me at a Strip club where I used to solicit my body for money. Why didn't you call the police on the club owners, they were pimping on me wasn't they?!" Waving her right hand like she doesn't want any more desert Christy says, "You will just never let that go, will you? I told you I was sorry, I told you a thousand times I didn't know what he was going to do. I thought he was just going to make sure you were in good health." With a loud burst of hurt and anger Diamond screams, "You lie! You fuckin liar! You forced me to go into the room, when you knew muthafuckin well that fat ass man wasn't no dam doctor, you let him rape me bitch!" Trying to save face her mother interrupts her and says, "I was sick baby, I wasn't in my right mind, I would never let anyone harm my one and only daughter!" Diamond listened and said, "What the fuck you mean you was sick? If you were sick, you should've been the one to have played doctor with that nasty muthafucka!" Flat out her mother said straightforwardly, "I was a dope fiend Diamond okay, I was a crackhead, okay? are you happy now? your mother was a crack hoe selling her body just like you." Feeling relieved because she got that off her chest and finished by saying, "The man didn't want me because I was all used up and worn out. You were the only thing I had that that filthy man wanted to pay for." Christy started crying over the phone and Diamond was crying over the phone too. Christy said, "Baby I regret every second of that day, I felt so bad when he was finished, and I saw you crying. I didn't even smoke the drugs he left me because I was messed up by what I had did to you. The next day I dropped you off at your auntie's house and admitted myself to a sober living environment house and got my shit together baby. And I haven't used crack ever since, please forgive me." Diamond was still speechless and just continued to cry and sob over the phone. She was surely hurt about what her mother told her about being a crack hoe and selling her only daughter for crack to a stranger. She was also relieved that her mother got her act together and quit smoking because of that situation. "Baby is there anything that I can do to make it up to you?" said her mother, Christy sniffing. Still reeling from the bombshell of the entire conversation that she had with her mom, she started to cuss her out some more, but caught herself and said, "Mom there is nothing that you can do to take back that day and moment because it has already happened." I wrestle with this every day of my life, and it is imputed into my brain." Thinking fast Diamond said, "There are some things you can do to make things right." Not wanting to let her down her mother replied, "What is it baby? What is it I'll do what I can to make things right?!" While wiping her nose with a tissue and sniffling she says, "You can start by calling that police officer, and tell him you don't want to press charges on us, and that you were just upset at the time. Also, you can call Child Protective Services, and tell them you lied and filed a false report even if you left your name anonymous mom so that way, we won't be looking over our shoulders for them while we out here hustling." Shaking her head in agreement her mother accepts the mission and says, "Okay baby, I'll get right on it right now, so y'all won't have to worry but what about being wanted for murder?" Exhaling and having a better understanding with her mother Diamond says, "We'll deal with it, how he says we should." Christy now truly feeling a part of a team says, "OK, you guys be careful out there, and keep in touch with me so that I know nothing has happened to y'all alright baby?" Shaking her head in agreement with her mom Diamond says, "I will mom" the phone call ended.

54
CHAPTER
❖
IT'S ALL GOOD

Christy was able to get the police off our backs along with C.P.S. After her and Diamond kissed and made up, things been going cool for the both of them. I be giving Christy and Auntie a few dollars from time to time. I'm hot out here in Vegas now with my Harem and we making money baby. Diamond is still my main bitch, and she helps keep all the other hoes in line. There is a total of six that I have, and they are all gamed up and glad to be on my team. The hoes take shifts watching little man Braxton when his mother can't watch him. Some hoes come and some hoes go but the pimping stays the same. If a bitch of mine gets arrested or must go to a court date, I'm not even going. That's how they take pictures of you and start cases and profiles and bust pimps and shit. Smooth and I are still the dynamic duo of pimping. He got his weight up and his hoes are keeping him happy. Oh, I finally found out about what happened to Kay-Kay. Her cousin told me that they ended up in Los Angeles living near one of the many glorious beaches. She saved every penny, every dime, and every dollar, so that she could pay her "favorite man" back. She decided to send me my money and then some, to my mother's house in Oakland. She sent it first class federal express. Boo kidnapped her from her "favorite man", and he was trying to make me think that she stole my money and drugs and disappeared. Meanwhile, I got a call on my cellphone. "Hello" "What's up lil bro you out there in Vegas having it yo way and can't call nobody?" it was my oldest brother. I was hella juiced to hear from him and responded, "A big brah how you doing man? Naw it ain't like that at all, this pimpin has been hitting me in the face and I forgot to take some time out to check on everybody." Big Bruh said, "lil brah we know how it is when you're out there ripping and running, pimpin and gunning, don't trip, everybody is doing fine. Say man uh, it's a package here for you from that bitch Kay-Kay but it ain't no return address on it." I didn't expect a package especially from L.A. then Big Bruh said, "Dam I thought the bitch was still online I never knew she jumped ship. Well, it seems like the bitch is trying to reach out and touch you like AT&T with this package being mailed here." Big bruh said, "What happened between y'all two?" I responded, "It's a long story Big Bruh but go ahead and open that package and see what's in it for me?" Big Bruh opened the package and yelled "dam!" as loud as hell and dropped the phone. I was on the other line tripping like what could it be? Could it be a severed head or something? Big Bruh returned to the phone with a slight laugh and said, "Lil brah, the bitch done sent you the lottery through the mail. I see I taught you well with this pimpin didn't I?" Now my excitement has increased to a feverish pitch, and I asked, "What you mean the lottery big brah?" Big Bruh proudly stated, "This bitch done sent you a stack of hundred-dollar bills." He counted it for me, and it totaled forty-five thousand dollars. That means I got my twenty thousand dollars back and an extra twenty-five thousand. Now about starting my trucking company…

Printed in the United States
by Baker & Taylor Publisher Services